W9-AUM-033

ALSO BY CARLO D'ESTE

Decision in Normandy

Bitter Victory: The Battle for Sicily, 1943

World War II in the Mediterranean, 1942–1945

Fatal Decision: Anzio and the Battle for Rome

Patton: A Genius for War

Eisenhower

Eisenhower
A SOLDIER'S LIFE

CARLO D'ESTE

WEIDENFELD & NICOLSON

Weidenfeld & Nicolson
Wellington House, 125 Strand
London WC2R 0BB

First published in the USA by Henry Holt and Company, LLC, 2002
This edition 2003

British Library Cataloguing-in-Publication Data. A catalogue record for this book is available from the British Library.

ISBN 0-304-36604-8

Designed by Fritz Metsch
Maps by Paul Pugliese
Frontispiece photograph of Dwight Eisenhower, June 6, 1944, courtesy of the Library of Congress.

Printed and bound in Great Britain by Clays Ltd, St Ives plc

For

SHIRLEY ANN

with love

For

M. S. "BUZ" WYETH, JR.

one of the great editors of our time

In memory of my friend

DAVID S. TERRY,

World War II citizen-soldier, esteemed educator, talented musician, and one who made this world a better place

and

In memory of the victims of the outrage of September 11, 2001

Contents

IV. THE INTERWAR YEARS, 1920–39

V. THE UNITED STATES PREPARES FOR WAR, 1940–42

VI. A GENERAL'S EDUCATION: THE MEDITERRANEAN, 1942–43

Eisenhower

Prologue: “An Astonishing Man”

Dwight D. Eisenhower endured many dramatic, tension-filled days, but nothing ever exceeded the events leading up to his courageous decision to launch the greatest military invasion in the history of warfare on June 6, 1944. The outcome of the war hinged on its success. Failure was unthinkable but nevertheless entirely possible, as Eisenhower knew only too well.

More than 150,000 Allied troops, nearly six thousand ships of every description, and masses of military hardware were crammed on ships and landing craft, and on airfields, awaiting Eisenhower’s “Go” order to commence what he would later term “the great crusade,” the cross-Channel operation that was the necessary overture to victory in Europe.

At the last minute the forces of nature intervened when a full-blown gale swept in from the Atlantic Ocean, and on June 4 Eisenhower was forced to postpone D-Day, originally scheduled for June 5, for at least twenty-four hours while the weathermen consulted their charts and received new data before the next weather update. At 4:15 A.M. on the morning of June 5, 1944, the Allied commanders in chief met to learn if the invasion could take place or would have to be postponed indefinitely. When the meteorologists predicted a break in the weather just sufficient to mount the invasion, Eisenhower made a historic decision that set into motion the most vital Allied operation of World War II—the operation that would decide the victor and the vanquished. To go or not to go based on this small window of acceptable weather became the basis for a decision only Eisenhower himself could make. And make it he did, deciding that the invasion must be launched on June 6.

In public Eisenhower exuded confidence; in private, however, he was a seething bundle of nervous energy. “Ike could not have been more anxiety ridden,” noted his British chauffeur and confidante, Kay Summersby. His smoking had increased to four packs a day, and he was rarely seen without a cigarette in his hand. “There were smoldering cigarettes in every ashtray. He would light one, put it down, forget it, and light another.”[1] On this day, June 5, he drank one pot of coffee after another and was once heard to mutter, “I hope to God I know what I’m doing.” Time dragged interminably, each hour seeming as long as a day.

Early that evening, with only his British aide, Lt. Col. Jimmy Gault, for company, he had Kay Summersby drive him to Newbury, Wiltshire, where the U.S. 101st Airborne Division was staging for its parachute and glider landings in Normandy's Cotentin Peninsula that night to help protect the landings on Utah Beach. Beginning that afternoon, the division had marched to its loading sites to the strains of "A Hell of a Way to Die"—also known as "He Ain't Gonna Jump No More," the song was actually "The Battle Hymn of the Republic" with lyrics appropriate to paratroopers—played by the division band. Arriving unannounced, he ordered the four-star plate on the front of his automobile covered, and permitted only a single division officer to accompany him on a random stroll through the ranks of the paratroopers, their faces blackened, full combat packs weighing an average of 125 to 150 pounds littering the ground around them, as they awaited darkness and the signal to begin the laborious process of loading. Although Eisenhower never spoke or wrote much about the experience, he cannot have forgotten the ominous warnings of his air commander in chief, Air Chief Marshal Sir Trafford Leigh-Mallory, that he fully expected casualties among the men of the elite airborne to be prohibitively high.

In total informality Eisenhower wandered from group to group, as men crowded around him, anxious to meet the general known as Ike. As he moved among the ranks he would ask repeatedly, "Where are you from, soldier?" "What did you do in civilian life?" Back came replies from young men from virtually every state in the Union. Some joked with Eisenhower, others remained somber. One invited him to Texas to herd cattle at his ranch after the war. "They went crazy, yelling and cheering because 'Ike' had come to see them off."

Possibly the most famous photograph of Eisenhower taken during the war depicts him surrounded by "Screaming Eagles" (the 101st's nickname), as he questioned one of the jumpmasters, Lt. Wallace Strobel, who assured him that he and his men were ready to do the job they had been trained for. Strobel would later say of his brief encounter with the supreme Allied commander, "I honestly think it was his morale that was improved by being with us." Others interjected remarks such as, "Don't worry, General, we'll take care of this thing for you." As twilight settled over southern England, the men of the 101st began the tedious process of loading aboard their C-47s and gliders. Eisenhower went to the runway to see them off, wishing them good luck. Some saluted and had their salute returned. One paratrooper was heard to announce, "Look out, Hitler. Here we come!"[2]

In some respects the scene was surreal: brave young men, many of whom would be wounded and perish in the coming hours and days, camouflaging their natural fears with bravado; and their commander in chief, deeply cognizant of what he had wrought, concealing his apprehension with smiles and small talk. "It's very hard to look a soldier in the eye when you fear that you are sending him to his death," Eisenhower later related to Kay Summersby. Yet those who had seen or spoken with him that fateful night carried into battle a conviction that their top soldier cared personally about each of them.

By nightfall Eisenhower had visited three airfields, at each of which the cheering was repeated. "I found the men in fine fettle," he said, "many of them joshingly admonishing me that I had no cause for worry, since the 101st was on the job and everything would be taken care of in fine shape."[3] The last man to embark was the division commander, Maj. Gen. Maxwell D. Taylor, who would shortly parachute into a Normandy cow pasture. Eisenhower saluted Taylor's aircraft as it moved off to join the enormous queue awaiting takeoff.

The noise was deafening. Eisenhower and the members of his party climbed onto the roof of the division headquarters to watch in silence as hundreds of planes and gliders lumbered into the rapidly darkening sky, again saluting as each aircraft passed by. For Eisenhower, a man unused to expressing his emotions publicly, it was a painfully moving yet exhilarating experience, and the closest he would come to being one of them. NBC correspondent Merrill Mueller stood nearby and noted that Eisenhower, his hands deep in his pockets, had tears in his eyes.[4]

Eisenhower remained after the last aircraft had taken off and their sounds had faded away in the night. Watching him stroll back to his staff car, deep in thought, his shoulders sagging as they did whenever he was troubled, Kay Summersby thought him the loneliest man in the world at that moment. The knot of apprehension in his gut can only be imagined, but the expression on his face revealed more than words. "Well, it's on," he said somberly, again looking up at the night sky. "No one can stop it now."[5]

His birth name was David Dwight Eisenhower, but he was best known simply by his nickname, "Ike." Well before he became president of the United States, Dwight Eisenhower was already a national hero and one of the most universally respected Americans of his time. As his son, noted historian John S. D. Eisenhower, would later write of Gen. Winfield Scott, Dwight Eisenhower was "an astonishing man, one of the most astonishing in American history."[6]

His life was an amazing saga of the American dream come true. He came from humble, undistinguished midwestern roots, yet rose to a position undreamed of during the most destructive war in the history of mankind. The son of pacifists, he became a soldier whose life and career were shaped by the very wars his parents despised; yet he decried war as "the most stupid and tragic of human ventures."[7] Had he followed the destiny predicted for him when he graduated from high school in Abilene, Kansas, in 1909, Eisenhower would have taught history instead of making it.

In 1941, as the United States was being drawn into a world war with

Japan, Italy, and Nazi Germany, Eisenhower's aspirations were modest. An earlier biographer has observed that the first fifty-two years of Eisenhower's life were not only unexceptional, but in complete contradiction of the notion that a heroic life is one filled with dramatic and noteworthy feats.[8] He would have considered himself successful to have served as a mere colonel in an armored division under the command of his longtime friend, the flamboyant Gen. George S. Patton, Jr.

Instead he rose to the highest command accorded any soldier in the Western Alliance of World War II. The fate of the war against Germany fell on his shoulders in June 1944, a responsibility of awesome and terrifying potential for failure—one faced by few military commanders in history.

By the time Germany surrendered in May 1945 Eisenhower's name was known and acclaimed throughout the world. "He came home with the cheers of millions from London, Paris, New York, and Kansas City ringing in his ears, heavily laden with medals, citations, decorations and honors such as had been bestowed on no other American in history."[9] Yet, at a huge welcome ceremony, he said humbly to the citizens of his beloved hometown, "The proudest thing I can say today is that I am from Abilene."[10]

How much do we really know about Eisenhower? A great deal has been written about him, but surprisingly little of it reflects the anguish of high command or of the two decades of behind-the-scenes toil, study, and apprenticeship that helped to prepare him. Or of his debilitating health problems, any one of which might have ended his career. One of the questions this book seeks to answer is what it was like to have been the supreme Allied commander; to face problems that would have crushed a lesser man; to deal with the likes of Winston Churchill, George C. Marshall, Franklin Delano Roosevelt, and a host of British military men, more experienced than he was, including three field marshals—Harold Alexander, Alan Brooke, and the controversial Bernard Law Montgomery.

More than a half century later, it is still difficult to grasp fully the enormity of his responsibilities, and the pressures placed upon him, first in the Mediterranean and then later in England, where he faced the greatest test of all, the invasion of Normandy in June 1944. As the story of his life through 1945 is unveiled, it will become evident that no amount of training or experience could fully have prepared Dwight Eisenhower for his role in World War II. That he was equal to the task is now virtually taken for granted; however; during those desperate and bloody years nothing was certain. Indeed, on the basis of Eisenhower's first experiences in North Africa, many expected him to fail.

He may not have fitted the mold of the warrior hero or of a battlefield general in the tradition of Robert E. Lee, J. E. B. Stuart, Stonewall Jackson, or George S. Patton, yet he was every inch a soldier. His legacy is based on his molding an alliance of two prickly, independent-minded allies with fundamentally disparate philosophies of waging war. Many have been misled by Eisenhower's easygoing manner and charming smile, a disarming facade behind which lay a ruthless, ambitious officer who thirsted to advance his chosen career by answering the call to war, which eventually led him to the pinnacle of his profession as a soldier. Eisenhower's well-concealed but towering ambition, his lifetime of study and drive to succeed was, like Patton's, one of the best-kept secrets of his extraordinary success. His infectious grin may have been "worth an army corps in any campaign," as his wartime British subordinate Lt. Gen. Sir Frederick Morgan has said, "but mostly," notes historian Eric Larrabee, "it was a quality that Eisenhower himself went to some lengths to conceal from the public: intelligence, an intelligence as icy as has ever risen to the higher reaches of American life."[11]

The path from the poverty of turn-of-the-century Abilene, Kansas, to supreme Allied commander was as improbable as it was spectacular. Certainly the advent of the new millennium is an auspicious occasion to introduce Dwight Eisenhower to new generations of Americans who know too little of this remarkable man. In chronicling his life through World War II, I am mindful of the observation by Gen. Claire Chennault's biographer, Martha Byrd: "To write an individual's biography is a joy, a privilege and a sobering responsibility."[12]

Part I

THE EISENHOWERS, 1741–1909

History is lived forwards but it is written in retrospect. We know the end before we consider the beginning and we can never wholly recapture what it was to know the beginning only.

—C. V. WEDGWOOD
William the Silent

1.

"Say Eisenhauer for Ironcutter."

They were believers in the doctrine of Menno Simons, who preached no authority outside the Bible.

Dwight D. Eisenhower's first ancestor in America was Hans Nicholas Eisenhauer, who emigrated from Germany's Rhineland to Pennsylvania in 1741. As the name was then spelled, it meant "iron hewer" or "iron cutter."

According to family lore, some of the earliest Eisenhauers may have been medieval warriors, dating possibly to the time of Charlemagne, who lived in Bavaria's Odenwald farming region. Over time the Eisenhauers evolved from warriors into pacifists. Many German Protestants at the time were followers of the doctrine of Menno Simons, the Swiss founder of the Mennonite movement, who preached in 1528 that no authority, either religious or political, existed other than the Bible and personal conscience. Simons advocated pacifism and urged his followers to reject the evils of materialism, proclaiming that "the true Christian should make no compromise with the world . . . [but] follow the dictates of his own conscience, inspired and guided by the Word of God."

Among the disciples of the Mennonite movement were Dwight Eisenhower's ancestors, who were undoubtedly among those victimized during the Thirty Years' War (1618–48) for their beliefs. The movements of the Eisenhauers during this time are unclear, but the family is thought to have fled to Switzerland for sanctuary at some point. By the eighteenth century, religious persecution, lawlessness, plagues, and pestilence had become the stimulus for a great many Europeans to seek a better life in the British New World colonies. Many were persuaded to emigrate by William Penn, the founder and first governor of the Quaker colony called Pennsylvania, which had also become a haven for all other persecuted religious sects. Although Penn's new colony had a great deal to offer, it was populated mainly by craftsmen and merchants and seriously lacked the skills of farmers to till the land and produce the food needed for survival. In the 1740s this void led Penn to Germany's Rhineland, where he gave speeches encouraging German Protestant farmers to emigrate to Pennsylvania with glowing tales of its spiritual riches and its arable lands.

"The result was a flood of emigration from Germany to Pennsylvania, of which the Eisenhauers were to become a part."[1]

The earliest identifiable ancestor was Hans Peter Eisenhauer of Elterbach in the Rhineland. His youngest son was Hans Nicholas Eisenhauer, who left Rotterdam aboard the sailing ship *Europa*, arriving in Philadelphia on November 20, 1741. After swearing the required oath of allegiance to both the British Crown and the Commonwealth of Pennsylvania, the Eisenhauer family settled in Bethel Township, near Harrisburg. On January 20, 1753, Hans Nicholas purchased a 168-acre farm, which "was recorded under the name of Nicholas Ironcutter. The clerk wrote on the draft: 'Say Eisenhauer for Ironcutter.' "[2] It would be two hundred years later to the day that Hans Nicholas's great-great-great grandson was inaugurated as the thirty-fourth president of the United States.

Upon his death, Hans Nicholas deeded the farm to his eldest son, John Peter Eisenhauer, also known as Peter Ironcutter, who became a successful farmer and merchant in nearby Fredericksburg, Pennsylvania. John Peter Eisenhauer died in 1802 at the age of seventy-eight, the same year Frederick, the youngest of his seventeen children, was born. The second of Eisenhauer's sons to be named Frederick, he was the great grandfather of Dwight D. Eisenhower.

Frederick was both a farmer and a weaver, and breaking with the tradition of large families, he and his wife, Barbara Miller, produced a mere six children. Before Frederick, little is known of the religious practices of the first Eisenhowers in America other than that they were predominantly Lutheran. Barbara Miller, who brought a generous dowry to their marriage, belonged to the church of the River Brethren, which Frederick joined in 1816.

The River Brethren, officially organized in 1862 as the Brethren in Christ, were a fundamentalist sect of the Mennonites, who had broken with their order as a result of religious quarrels.[3]

One of Frederick's sons, the Reverend Jacob Eisenhower, was Dwight Eisenhower's grandfather, and the most dynamic and admired of his ancestors. A devoutly religious farmer, Jacob purchased one hundred acres of prime land outside Elizabethville, in the lush Lykens Valley, some twenty-five miles northwest of Harrisburg in an area that was home to many of the River Brethren.

Practicing what they preached, the Eisenhowers graciously opened their spacious, nine-room manor house to travelers, vagrants, and anyone in need of food and shelter. The large living room also doubled as a place of worship and communion for members of the Reverend Mr. Eisenhower's flock. It was here that Eisenhower, an acclaimed orator who sported a beard around his chin but had his upper lip clean-shaven in the manner of the Puritans and the Pennsylvania Amish community, delivered his sermons in German, which was still the mother tongue of most of Elizabethville's citizenry. Years later, his grandson, Edgar Eisenhower, would remember how Jacob spoke "with a broken Pennsylvania Dutch brogue."[4]

Several Eisenhower relatives are known to have served the Union during the Civil War, but Jacob Eisenhower himself took no part. The war posed a troubling dilemma for Jacob, who neither condemned nor endorsed the Union but so greatly admired President Lincoln that he named one of his sons Abraham.

Before Kansas became a state, most maps showed the region west of the town of Manhattan as uncharted territory. On some maps it was marked the "Great American Desert."[5] In 1877, some of the River Brethren, no doubt lured by advertisements that promised bountiful crops and newspaper articles praising the richness of the land and its open spaces, ventured to Kansas to see for themselves. They arrived at the peak of the harvest season and found an area of rich soil capable of producing large crops, orchards, grass for cattle, unspoiled rivers, and stands of adequate timber along the creeks and rivers. Their reports of life in Kansas were so encouraging that within the River Brethren community there was discussion of relocating the entire sect to Dickinson County, considered the best of the sites investigated. This led to a momentous group decision by many of the Brethren voluntarily to give up their homes and farms in Pennsylvania and move en masse to a promised but largely unknown land in Middle America.

The westward expansion of the United States was spurred by the explosive growth of the railroads. Between 1865 and 1880, the American railway system grew from thirty-five to ninety-three thousand miles, and in 1869, the transcontinental railway was completed in Utah with the symbolic ceremony of the golden spike.

The lure of the great American West was bolstered by Lincoln's major land reform, the Homestead Act of 1862, which granted 160 acres of land to each new settler and hastened the demise of the traditional Indian lands. Inexorably the tribes were forced into reservations as white ranchers took over the fertile land and erected fences, while farmers began to make use of new farming machinery pioneered by John Deere.[6] The subjugation of the western Indian tribes may have been inevitable, but their shameful mistreatment was also one of the great tragedies of American history.

With the age of the railroad in Texas still some years away, the only means Texas cattlemen had of reaching a market was via the trail drive along the dusty Chisholm Trail into Kansas, across what is now Oklahoma but in the 1860s was still called Indian Territory.[7]

Between 1867 and 1885 Kansas became the ideal location to which the Texas herds could be driven and sold to livestock brokers. Among the first to realize the profit potential of buying and selling cattle to the lucrative eastern markets was a young Springfield, Illinois, livestock entrepreneur named Joseph G. McCoy, who sought a suitable location in Kansas "undisturbed by mobs or swindling thieves."[8] McCoy chose the tiny village of Abilene, where an extension of the Chisholm Trail terminated, as did the Kansas Pacific Railroad, which reached the town in March 1867.[9]

When McCoy established residence in 1867 he described Abilene as a "small, dead place consisting of about one dozen log huts" with dirt roofs, and a single saloon keeper who maintained a colony of prairie dogs with which he supplemented his income by selling them as curiosities to eastern tourists. Nevertheless McCoy deemed Abilene an ideal site, not only for its location but also for its grasslands and excellent water supply. Determined to turn Abilene into a thriving railhead cattle town, in a mere sixty days McCoy built stockyards large enough to hold a thousand head of cattle. Soon cattlemen began diverting their herds to Abilene.

Abilene quickly numbered some three thousand inhabitants as the trappings of a busy trading post sprang up almost overnight, bringing to the burgeoning town traders, merchants, gamblers, cardsharps, outlaws, assorted riffraff, and most of all, cowboys anxious, after the hardships of the trail, to enjoy home cooking and to patronize the saloons, dance halls, and whorehouses.[10] Most of Abilene's commerce was situated on Texas Street, which ran parallel to the Kansas Pacific tracks. Later, the action shifted to sin-filled districts called by various names, such as "Hell's Half-Acre," "Texas Town," and the "Devil's Addition," where about one hundred prostitutes plied their trade. One Abilene resident described the garishness of the "Devil's Addition" as "rightly named, for Hell reigned there. . . . in that damned Valley of Perdition." In July 1868 a Topeka newspaper observed, "Hell is now in session in Abilene."[11]

The term "Wild West" was coined in Kansas, and there was no cattle town wilder than Abilene in its heyday. In its infancy Abilene was a thoroughly inhospitable place: dusty and hellishly hot in summer and forbiddingly cold in winter, its streets a sea of mud whenever it rained. From the time that Joseph McCoy had put Abilene on the map, the town had endured a reign of terror by unruly roughnecks who jeeringly defied the town's attempts to control them. Its first lawmen either quit or were hounded out of town. No one paid the slightest attention to a new city ordinance banning guns, and as soon as a jail was constructed, it was torn down by a group of carousing cowboys. Killings and violence became so commonplace that even by the town's pinnacle in 1871 the founder of Abilene's first newspaper characterized the place as having more desperadoes than any other town of comparable size in the United States.[12]

In 1870, in an attempt to bring Abilene's lawlessness under control, the mayor hired a soft-spoken, fearless marshal named Thomas J. "Bear River Tom" Smith, a former New York City cop turned frontier lawman. Smith quickly lived up to his lofty reputation and during his brief tenure there were no more killings in Abilene. What made Tom Smith so unique was that he used his fists rather than guns to tame the town. In November 1870, Smith was brutally executed near Abilene while attempting to arrest two farmers. Tom Smith was followed for a short time by the notorious Wild Bill Hickok, who kept the peace in Abilene and killed his share of lawbreakers who dared to challenge his authority.[13]

In the post–Civil War period Abilene represented the best and worst of a growing and expanding America. Both Billy the Kid and Wyatt Earp are known to have passed through Abilene (without incident) during its brief reign as the West's wildest town. "Abilene was corruption personified," wrote one historian. "Life was hectic, raw, lurid, awful."[14]

In September 1867 the first cattle were shipped from Abilene to Chicago and put Abilene on the map.[15] During Abilene's heyday, between 1876 and 1879, 1,046,732 head of cattle were shipped east. In the end, however, McCoy lost money in Abilene, and moved on. The ultimate irony was that the strongly religious McCoy utterly detested the violence and wickedness he had helped create in Abilene.

Abilene's tenuous monopoly as a cattle town and sin city lasted barely four years, and by 1872 it had fallen victim to the westward extension of the railroads, and the opposition of its now largely farming citizenry, who declared that "the inhabitants of Dickinson [County] . . . will no longer submit to the evils of the [cattle] trade."[16] Other sites, such as Wichita, Salina, and Ellsworth, soon flourished as cattle towns, their proliferation fueled by the emergence of a powerful rival to the Kansas Pacific: the Atchison, Topeka & Santa Fe Railway. By 1875 Dodge City had superseded Abilene in notoriety thanks to such colorful Western characters as Wyatt Earp, Billy Tilghman, Bat Masterson, Buffalo Bill Cody, John Wesley Hardin, and Doc Holliday.[17]

In the aftermath of its glory days, Abilene had, by the early 1880s, evolved into a typical Kansas agricultural town that catered to farmers and ranchers. Dickinson County began attracting land speculators; they bought up parcels of unimproved land, divided them into lots, and advertised in eastern newspapers to attract settlers anxious to find new lives in the West. An 1887 brochure luridly proclaimed that "Abilene is to be a city of ten thousands in a few years," with "factories, fine business blocks, beautiful homes," and even a streetcar line. Another advertised that Abilene "has all the right stuff."[18] Dwight Eisenhower would later write, "Civic pride, in many American towns of that period, was the most flourishing local industry."[19] Although Abilene ultimately turned out to be a bad investment for the speculators (who outnumbered buyers by the late 1880s), it brought settlers keen to take advantage of the Homestead Act. So rapid was Abilene's evolution from Wild West town to agrarian center that the River Brethren, undeterred by its violent reputation, began to settle in Dickinson County less than a decade after Joseph McCoy had turned Abilene into "America's first great cowtown."[20]

2.

The Promised Land

They were good people.
—MILTON S. EISENHOWER

In the year 1878, Jacob Eisenhower and his family were part of a migration to Dickinson County, Kansas, that numbered several hundred Pennsylvania River Brethren. The Eisenhowers arrived in Abilene in April in the first group and settled some twelve miles southeast of Abilene, where he purchased 160 acres of prime farmland. For nearly a year the Eisenhowers lived in a covered wagon while Jacob built a spacious new home for his family.[1]

It did not take long for the River Brethren to validate the wisdom of their decision to leave Pennsylvania. Even during the depression years of the late 1880s and the 1890s, they prospered in Kansas. Corn, hay, wheat, barley, and oats were staples, and their large herds of cows almost always produced a surplus of milk. Their cooperative religious spirit also extended to economic matters, in which the River Brethren proved to be shrewd businessmen.

In 1886 the sect established the Belle Springs Creamery near Jacob Eisenhower's farm.[2] The creamery skimmed butterfat from milk and paid dividends based on each farmer's contribution. It proved to be an enormously important addition to the economic well-being of the farmers of Dickinson County. In 1890 the creamery was moved to Abilene, where it became a major factor in the lives of the Eisenhowers and a vital economic component of the Abilene community, both for its output and as a significant source of employment.[3]

In a profession fraught with risk and failure, Jacob Eisenhower was even more successful in Kansas than he had been in Pennsylvania. The family's lives revolved around crops and religion. They worked six days a week tilling the land; on the seventh day Jacob preached to the assembled River Brethren in his grand new home. Within a few years he was sufficiently affluent to invest in a team of fast ponies, a small county bank, and to purchase real estate in Hope, Kansas, then a tiny village near the family homestead in Belle Springs. The success that Jacob enjoyed in Kansas also promised a similarly good life for his children. Although strict and demanding, Jacob was also exceedingly generous. When his children married each received two thousand dollars in cash and a quarter section of farmland (160 acres).

Farming did not appeal to Jacob's eldest surviving son, dark-haired, brooding David Jacob Eisenhower, who was born in 1863.[4] His father's success at farming and modest wealth notwithstanding, David Eisenhower was at a rebellious and restless age, and filled with dreams, few of which seemed rooted in reality. He despised farming and had for some time been steadfastly determined not to carry on the family tradition, which he found tedious and unrewarding. David's only known aspirations were to become an engineer and a successful businessman. Although he delighted in using his hands, especially to repair farm machinery, David was scholarly, contemplative, and possessed of an inquiring and restless mind. He learned to read Greek for his own enjoyment, and his sons later recalled him reading the Bible in Greek, which was the only version he seemed to trust. He has been described as having unusually large hands, a thick shock of black hair, and was "tall and muscular, with the broad shoulders that characterized all Eisenhower men."[5] David also possessed in abundance the Eisenhower trait of stubbornness.

The United Brethren in Christ were another of the evangelical fundamentalist sects that abounded in Kansas, and their religious doctrine was more Methodist than Baptist. Although Lane emphasized religious education, the university offered both liberal arts and vocational training.[6] The entire school consisted of ten instructors and a small student body of approximately two hundred.[7]

David studied Greek, rhetoric, mechanics, and mathematics, and soon met his future wife, a vivacious young woman named Ida Elizabeth Stover, whose ancestors had emigrated from Europe two hundred years earlier for the same reasons as the Eisenhowers. Ida was born May 1, 1862, in Mount Sidney, Virginia, a tiny township in the Shenandoah Valley near Staunton, the next to youngest and the only girl of the eight children of Simon P. and Elizabeth Link Stover. Originally christened in the Lutheran Church as Elizabeth Ida, she later reversed her names, just as she would one day do for her famous son.[8]

Ida Stover—who was fondly remembered as a young girl of great charm and brightness—grew up with strong religious convictions and a pacifism powerfully influenced by painful memories of slavery and war. After the death of her mother in 1867, her father was unable to cope with raising so many children, and in 1869 sent seven-year-old Ida to live with her maternal grandfather, William Link. After Simon Stover died in 1873, William Link became Ida's guardian. She chafed at her grandfather's disdain for higher learning by women, something he—like most men of his time—regarded as unnecessary and unladylike. The adventuresome Ida refused to be deterred from her burning ambition to achieve a proper education, with or without permission. At age eighteen she left home to attend high school in Staunton and earned money for her keep by baking pies and cooking in private homes, a skill she had been perfecting since the age of seven. Ida's studies included the Bible, and she once memorized 1,365 biblical verses, any of which she could freely quote.[9] During her last two years in Virginia, Ida taught in a one-room schoolhouse near Mount Sidney.

At age twenty-one Ida received a one-thousand-dollar inheritance left by her late father and decided to join several of her brothers, who were part of the great Kansas migration. In June 1883 Ida settled in Lecompton with her elder brother William, a preacher.[10]

Ida's greatest passion was music, so much so that she spent six hundred dollars of her precious dowry for an ebony piano, which, to the end of her life, would remain her most cherished possession. Now free to make her own decisions, Ida enrolled in nearby Lane University in the autumn of 1883 to take advantage of its courses in music and the liberal arts.[11]

Early photographs depict a self-assured, attractive young woman. There were few women at Lane, and the golden-blond-haired Ida quickly became an extremely popular student, as well as the object of attention from young men anxious to win her approval. Ida did not meet David Eisenhower until the autumn of 1884, David's first year at Lane. At first David showed interest in several other female students, each of whom rebuffed his advances. Before long, however, David and Ida began attending various school functions together. If there is truth in the adage that opposites attract, it certainly applied to David Eisenhower and Ida Elizabeth Stover.

Young Ida Stover's personality and traits were everything David's were not: She was witty, popular, vivacious, and outgoing. David was considered by his peers at Lane to be as disagreeable as Ida was well-liked. A fellow student has painted an unflattering portrait of David, noting that when he enrolled at Lane he was cocky, very smart, with an extremely large ego and an inflated opinion of himself. "He *never* quit loving himself . . . but after awhile he settled down and found he was as common as an old shoe." One evening David was so rude to Ida at a student social that he was firmly rebuked by a number of his classmates, giving him to understand "that they would not tolerate his ugly attitude toward Ida . . . after that he seemed to try to please her and be somewhat human."[12]

David's behavior may occasionally have been insensitive, but it did not deter Ida from becoming deeply attracted to the handsome young man whose intellect far outweighed his introverted nature. What had begun as an instant attraction rapidly evolved into a serious courtship. David became a frequent visitor to the Link household. Ida's cousin Nettie Stover recalled how, at ten P.M. one night, William's second wife, Annie, bluntly announced, "It's time all decent folks were home in bed." David regarded the rebuke as a personal affront and vowed "to fix it so nobody was telling him when he had to leave."[13]

(One of David's traits was indecisiveness, at least until he made up his mind; then he became single-minded and beyond persuasion. Neither trait would necessarily serve him well.)

According to Nettie Stover the incident merely served to intensify David's courtship of Ida, although he never again returned to Will Stover's home until the day of his wedding to Ida, on his twenty-second birthday, September 23, 1885. Significantly the ceremony was performed not by Jacob Eisenhower or Will Stover, but by a River Brethren minister, E. B. Slade, in the presence of twenty guests.[14]

Whether David and Ida were true River Brethren remains in considerable doubt, however. According to David's nephew, the Reverend Ray Witter, neither David nor Ida ever became full-fledged members of the sect, even though they supported its basic tenets, sent their sons to its Sunday school, and attended its religious services until 1895. Another family friend confirms that he "never knew any of the family to attend the River Brethren Church." Both were perhaps too independent-minded to have sustained a permanent affiliation. Dwight Eisenhower would later describe his parents as "somewhat rebellious" in their approach to religion, and "not easily satisfied with any church."[15]

To support a wife, David had decided that his future lay in the mercantile and grocery business. He approached his father, offering to trade his inheritance for a start-up loan to open a store in Hope. The price of opening the store required that David bargain away his farm. Having rejected farming for business, the young couple were obliged to quit Lane University. David withdrew, probably in early 1885, followed by Ida at the end of the 1884–85 school year.

The year before Jacob had given two thousand dollars and a farm to David's older sister Amanda when she wed Christian O. Musser, a young member of the River Brethren who had migrated to Kansas from Pennsylvania in March 1884. Chris Musser regularly attended Jacob Eisenhower's Sunday services, where he met and courted Amanda, whom he married six months later. Chris Musser used Amanda's dowry wisely, and in later years the couple became two of Abilene's most prominent citizens, farming families, and business successes.

When David asked his father for a loan, Jacob agreed to mortgage the farm he intended to deed to his son. According to Musser, Jacob approached him to ask "if I could get some money from Pennsylvania for [David] to go into the mercantile and grocery business." Chris Musser's uncle bought the mortgage for two thousand dollars, and Jacob used the proceeds to construct a two-story store on a vacant lot he owned in Hope.

David lacked business acumen and, very likely at the urging of his father, elected to take in a partner named Milton D. Good, a highly regarded, congenial salesman in an Abilene clothing store, once described in the *Hope*

Dispatch as "one of the best merchants who ever measured off a piece of bacon or weighed a yard of calico."

Milton Good and David Eisenhower thus became equal partners in the fledging business that opened its doors as the Good & Eisenhower Store in March 1885. The store had two apartments upstairs—one for David and his new bride, and the other for his newly acquired partner.

Young David and Ida Eisenhower could hardly have been more mismatched in personality and temperament. David was introspective, reclusive, a dreamer, and utterly lacking a sense of humor. He also possessed a violent temper and was given to fits of rage over the commission of sins (real or imagined) by others, including members of his own family. His admirable traits of decency notwithstanding, throughout his life David remained the same incommunicative person who was described so unflatteringly by his Lane University classmates.

Ida promptly learned how to overcome David's bullheadedness. Shortly after settling into their first home above the store in Hope, Ida said David would have to help her fix a balky window shade. "I don't have to do anything," he replied, ignoring her request. Instead of expressing anger, Ida calmly outwitted her husband. The next time she announced, "Dave, I wonder if you could do this: I can't seem to get it done." At once David leaped to do her bidding. It was a lesson she later used to great effect raising her sons, whom she taught that there was more than one way to overcome a problem.[16] However, when it came to the family finances, Ida willingly deferred that right and responsibility to her husband.

Like other women of the Kansas River Brethren, Ida adapted the traditional garb, which consisted of a long black dress with a matching black cape and apron, called a "frock and yock." On her head she wore a white cap called a "prayer covering," which was only removed for sleeping or combing. No jewelry or other adornments were permitted. After a time Ida asserted her independence by becoming only the second woman in the Belle Springs sect permanently to discard the traditional headgear.[17]

The new business prospered at first, far better than relations between the two partners. The accepted but apocryphal version passed down by David Eisenhower and his sons is that the store failed in 1887 or 1888, and Milton Good and his wife absconded with all the store's cash and were never seen again, leaving David Eisenhower a ruined man, responsible for its debts, which he turned over to a lawyer who Ida later believed had also cheated them.

This tale never had a factual basis and is founded solely on Eisenhower family lore. The fiction of Good's alleged treachery was passed down to David and Ida's sons, who accepted it as fact. The truth of what actually occurred was not revealed until 1990, when Thomas Branigar, a historian-archivist at the Eisenhower Presidential Library in Abilene, published an illuminating investigative article about David Eisenhower and Milton Good.[18]

The Good & Eisenhower Store did not fail, it was dissolved by mutual consent. The only failure was the incompatibility of the two partners after just eighteen months in business together. David mortgaged the entire stock of the store to his father for $3,500 and used the money to buy out Milton Good's share of the partnership on November 4, 1886. The official notice posted by David in the next day's edition of the *Hope Dispatch* stated that Milton Good was released "from all responsibilities of the late firm."[19] Three days later Jacob Eisenhower forgave David his obligation to repay the debt.

The heroic portrayal of David Eisenhower's alleged travails with Milton Good and how he spent years repaying his debts was a fantasy perpetuated and later embellished by his famous third son, Dwight, in his best-selling memoir, *At Ease: Stories I Tell to Friends.*

Not only was there no bankruptcy, but the store was reorganized and renamed "Eisenhower Brothers" when David's younger brother, Abraham, a River Brethren preacher and self-taught veterinarian, became his new partner. Abe Eisenhower was a character as outgoing as David was introverted. He loved horses and people with equal passion, and despite a lack of formal training and professional skills, made up for them with, as his grandson remembered well, "boundless energy and showmanship." To encourage the local farmers to seek his services, Abe would dash madly around the countryside in a two-wheeled buggy as if responding to a veterinary emergency. The ruse worked, and Abe was praised in the local paper for having "extraordinary luck with his veterinary practice."[20]

David's final two years in the business were marked by the same traits of unhappiness and barely concealed resentments that had characterized his short, unfortunate partnership with Milton Good. David clashed with a tenant who briefly operated a bakery in the Eisenhower building. Like so many other small businessmen of that era, the tenant, E. A. Gehrig, found himself in financial straits in early 1888. Soon rumors began spreading in Hope that Gehrig had been forced into bankruptcy by his creditors. The source was a vindictive David Eisenhower, who was still angry at Gehrig for moving his bakery. To defend himself Gehrig felt obliged to place a public notice in the April 7, 1887, edition of the *Hope Herald:* "The report that I have been closed was given circulation by David Eisenhower, whose malice toward me, because I recently moved from his building, is a matter of general knowledge."[21]

Contrary, too, to the family myth, Milton Good did not flee Dickinson County with the firm's cash. Instead, Good returned to Abilene in 1886, where he was active in town affairs. He opened a dry-goods store in 1892 at the worst of economic times.

. . .

A restless David Eisenhower quit his job at the Eisenhower Brothers general store in October 1888, just as his rapidly growing family was about to include its second child. In light of his family responsibilities, his decision is utterly incomprehensible, but it was not impulsive. To the contrary, David had long since lost interest in running the store.[22]

Now that he was jobless, it became imperative that David find work. Broke and clearly discouraged, David elected to leave Hope. One of his son's first biographers notes, "In self-violation, in violation of the frontier tradition of courage and self-reliance . . . he sought only to escape from the scene of his humiliation."[23] David may well have felt mortified, but it had nothing whatsoever to do with his alleged business failure or his debts. It is more likely that David Eisenhower was simply unable to cope with his own sense of failure. Neither parent ever revealed the truth to their sons, who went to their own graves believing that their father had been the victim of Milton Good's treachery. In so doing, Ida became her husband's accomplice, repeating the tale, Dwight remembers, "many times" to the Eisenhower children.[24] What is indisputable is that David Eisenhower left Ida and their firstborn son, Arthur, in the care of his brother Abe while he traveled to Texas in search of work.

Scarcely three years into their marriage, Ida was compelled to cope with the baby; a second pregnancy, then in its sixth month; and the unhappiness of being forsaken by her husband. In January 1889 Ida delivered a second son, Edgar, named in honor of Edgar Allan Poe. Years later, when her sons reminded her that Poe had been an alcoholic, she replied, "I don't care. I still like his poems."[25]

In February 1889 Jacob Eisenhower decided to move his family to Abilene, and soon afterward the store was sold to the owners of an Abilene hardware store after Abe too elected to leave Hope and follow his parents to Abilene after disposing of his veterinary business.[26] Their decision was undoubtedly buttressed by David's flight to Texas.

The southern terminus of the Missouri, Kansas & Texas Railway was the bustling railroad town of Denison, Texas.[27] Known colloquially as the Katy Railroad, then simply as the Katy, at its zenith it was linked to five other railway systems. The most significant date in Denison's history was an equally important one in that of the United States. On March 10, 1873, the first train arrived in Denison, which—the city's historian notes—"was more significant than the event in Utah . . . all of the United States—North, South, East and West—were linked for the first time by the steel bands of the railroad."[28]

It was the emergence of the Katy that lured David Eisenhower to Denison in October 1888, where he was hired as a lowly engine wiper for the grand sum of ten dollars per week. David rented a room in a nearby boardinghouse and lived frugally and alone. Perhaps to assuage his loneliness, David turned to religious mysticism for spiritual guidance and solace. He designed an enormous wall chart of the Egyptian pyramids, complete with lines, angles, and captions to which he assigned symbolic meanings. The chart was an amazingly original, if incomprehensible, work that endlessly fascinated his sons.[29] Throughout his life the reserved David remained a man of few words. Dwight Eisenhower's son, John, thought that "Granddad was something else," recalling the occasion when his father received a postcard from David that said simply, "Hot."[30]

In 1888 David Eisenhower was twenty-five years old and utterly miserable. The Denison years of his self-imposed exile, between October 1888 and March 1892, were undoubtedly the most dismal period of his life. He labored for minimal wages and in total obscurity "somewhere near the bottom of the American heap, without any discernible future."[31]

When Abe Eisenhower left Hope to join his father, Jacob, in Abilene in April 1889, Ida, Arthur, and the newborn Edgar were reunited with David, who rented a modest, run-down wood-frame house on the wrong side of the tracks in a working-class section of Denison, a few blocks from the Katy railroad yards. Soot from passing trains coated the tiny house, which the Eisenhowers shared with a boarder, James Redmon, a Katy engineer who lived upstairs. The railroad tracks were dangerously close to the home and no place for young children to play. So grave was their poverty in Denison that it was a luxury when Ida occasionally bought hot tamales, which were sold six for five cents by a local peddler.[32]

When his mother, Rebecca, died in June 1890 at the age of seventy-five, David left Ida (then five months pregnant with their third child) and Edgar in Denison and returned to Abilene for her funeral, bringing with him young Arthur Eisenhower. David's mournful trip merely reinforced his sense of loneliness at being far from his family.

Despite their obvious discontent, the Eisenhowers had scant time for reflection as the birth of their next child drew near. The imminent arrival of yet another mouth to feed on his miserable salary only deepened David's gloom. Moreover, with two boys already, the Eisenhowers understandably hoped that their next child would be a girl. It was not to be.

Named in honor of his father, David Dwight, the third Eisenhower son, was born under the sign of Libra on the night of October 14, 1890, during a violent Texas thunderstorm. When Ida went into labor, James Redmon, who happened to be home, was sent to summon a physician. Before he arrived, the child was born with the assistance of neighbors, who had crowded into the tiny house in the spirit of communal cooperation. Brother Edgar later jokingly noted that Dwight was the only member of the family born outside Kansas. "There he was, a renegade Texan in a family of Kansans."[33]

Ida abhorred the notion that her third son would undoubtedly be referred to as David Eisenhower, Jr., or nicknamed "Dave," and soon reversed his names ("Dwight" was given in honor of a leading evangelist of the time, Dwight Moody.) No birth certificate was ever officially recorded for Eisenhower, and the transposition of his two first names was strictly at his mother's whim. Nonetheless, his name appears in the family Bible as "David Dwight Eisenhower."[34]

Dwight Eisenhower had no recollection and only scant knowledge of his birthplace until June 1945, when a delegation from Denison traveled to Abilene to present him with a framed photograph of the house where he was born. The following year he made the first of two visits to Denison, but overall Eisenhower never evinced more than polite interest in his birthplace. As far as he was concerned, Abilene was his only home and Denison little more than a bad memory in his parents' lives.

Yet another of the myths about Eisenhower is that he always believed he had been born in the East Texas town of Tyler, where his father was alleged to have worked briefly before moving to Denison. David, however, never worked in Tyler, and when Dwight entered West Point in 1911 he correctly entered "Denison, Texas," as his birthplace on the admissions form.[35]

Arthur would later recall the profound sense of gloom that pervaded the Eisenhower home whenever the subject of Kansas arose, which was apparently often. "God himself is the only one who knows how our parents managed to feed five mouths on dad's salary," wrote Edgar.[36]

The Texas years had not only mellowed David but infused him with a genuine awareness of just how deeply he and his family missed Kansas. After the death of his wife, Jacob Eisenhower was himself increasingly lonely. In the spring of 1891 he visited Denison and returned home visibly shaken by the unhappiness of David and his family. Hints continued from Abilene that the family should return, but without the certainty of a job, David hesitated until Chris Musser, now the foreman at the Belle Springs Creamery, let it be known that a job awaited him.[37]

In March 1892, nearly three and a half years after David Eisenhower had left Hope, the exile ended when the family returned to Abilene and were reunited with Jacob and Uncle Abe. On the day they arrived, David Eisenhower's sole assets amounted to the $24.15 in his pocket.[38] Two blocks south of the Union Pacific tracks, David rented a tiny house that was barely one step above a shanty. It was all he could afford on his meager salary. For the next six years it would be home to his rapidly expanding family.[39]

For Ida it meant more than a homecoming. During her three years in Texas her cherished ebony piano had been left in the care of a friend in Abilene. Now she would have it back. David, Ida (once again pregnant with what would be their fourth son, Roy), Arthur, Edgar, and baby Dwight David had returned to the Kansas town that would forever be linked with the Eisenhower name.

3.

"A Good Place for Boys to Grow into Men"

Our lives as youngsters were full and purposeful.

—EDGAR EISENHOWER

Dwight Eisenhower's childhood resembled the quintessential depictions of rural American youth in the paintings of Norman Rockwell. Milton recalls that his older brother was "just about the most normal boy" imaginable.[1] Baseball was Dwight's true love, and his boyhood sports hero was the great Pittsburgh Pirates Hall of Fame shortstop, Honus Wagner. "Edgar, Roy and I, we could make a third of a team ourselves and we'd get over here in the schoolground and we would play every minute that we could possibly get . . . the life of all us boys together was more of fun and frolic than it was just drudgery. . . . We felt that we had a pretty good thing going here."[2]

Whenever he was not in school or working, young Eisenhower could be found sipping a sundae at Case's Department Store, riding precariously on the handlebars of a friend's bicycle, wading or fishing in nearby Mud Creek, shooting rabbits, general horseplay, engaging in fisticuffs, or competing in all manner of sports. There was little his boyhood in Abilene had to offer that Dwight Eisenhower did not take part in during an untroubled youth. The Eisenhowers could not afford toys, but with David's encouragement his sons became adept at manufacturing their own from whatever materials were handy. Camping and boating were all part of a life filled with activities, as were acrobatics and balancing acts in the family barn—often futile attempts to defy the laws of gravity that usually cost little more than numerous bumps, bruises, cuts, and scrapes. Whenever there was a water fight, young Eisenhower was certain to be an eager participant. Whether the fight was with relatives or friends, entire buckets of cold water were employed, usually flung directly into the face of the chosen victim. The boys had no bathing suits but swam anyway, as one friend recalled, "in nature's clothes," often paying for it later with a serious case of sunburn.[3]

Dwight sometimes rode his father's solid-tire bicycle or a horse, which was the primary means of travel in Abilene. With six active sons, Ida hastily developed impressive first-aid skills to treat their never-ending succession of minor injuries. She also developed an array of home remedies for virtually any occasion. Easily the most unpopular was a vile concoction of molasses and sulfur that Ida insisted on administering every spring. To enhance their iron levels, she also made her sons ingest gunpowder, which was highly unpopular. A never-opened bottle of whiskey was kept in the cupboard for medicinal purposes.[4]

Like the rest of the nation, the Eisenhower sons were captivated by the sinking of the battleship *Maine* in Havana harbor in 1898 and the heroic charge of Teddy Roosevelt's Rough Riders during the subsequent Spanish-American War. "Remember the *Maine*" and the Rough Riders became part of numerous imaginative childhood games played by the Eisenhowers. "A tiny knoll became San Juan Hill," where they "gallantly charged, fighting and dying gloriously. The mother, in one of her rare moments of interference with their play, strongly disapproved. For the first time they encountered her extreme pacifism as she lectured them on the wickedness of war. Thereafter the game of war was faintly flavored for them with the spice of sin."[5]

The sons of David and Ida Eisenhower grew up with an impressive array of skills that included forecasting the weather, telling time from the position of the sun, catching frogs, curing warts, making apple cider, wrestling, and, whenever (albeit rarely) possible, avoiding both work and soap and water. Loose teeth were dealt with by pulling out the offending tooth either with their own fingers or by means of a string tied to a doorknob, and fillings were the ingredients in pies, not teeth. What they lacked in material wealth they more than made up for in amusements and pranks. Edgar and Dwight were often the center of mischief, such as the occasions when they poured beer into a neighbor's hen to see its reaction or stripped someone's farm wagon and rebuilt it on the roof of their barn.

Dwight Eisenhower grew up with an affinity for his hometown that he never lost. His two enduring childhood fantasies were of being the engineer of a locomotive racing across the plains and arriving in Abilene with its bell clanging, or of being a fearless pitcher striking out the side with the bases loaded in the bottom of the ninth inning of a baseball game to the cheers of a great crowd of five hundred spectators.[6] The Abilene he knew at the turn of the century bore scant resemblance to the onetime Wild West town. One of young Eisenhower's boyhood heroes was Marshal Tom Smith. Not only in his youth did Eisenhower hear local tales of Smith's courage, but throughout his life he voraciously read stirring Western pulp novels. A favorite childhood game played by Dwight and Edgar was Wild West, in which they each played the role of Bat Masterson, Wild Bill Hickok, Jesse James, or perhaps Billy the Kid and had imaginary shoot-outs with equally make-believe six-shooters.

During World War II his enlisted orderly would regularly write to Mamie Eisenhower requesting Western novels, "preferably with a lot of shooting in them. It was sort of funny, considering the amount of shooting we were getting most nights, that he still wanted stories full of six-shooters and barroom brawls." With the advent of motion pictures, it was no coincidence that one of Eisenhower's all-time favorites was *High Noon*.[7]

Eisenhower frequently visited Smith's gravesite in Abilene, including three occasions during his presidency, taking inspiration from the words carved into the headstone:

THOMAS J. SMITH
Marshal of Abilene, 1870
Dead, a Martyr to Duty, Nov. 2, 1870.
A Fearless Hero of Frontier Days
Who in Cowboy Chaos
Established the Supremacy of Law.[8]

Eisenhower's first living boyhood hero was an Abilene resident named Bob Davis, whom he first met about 1898. Davis was a jack of all trades who earned his living as a fisherman, guide, and trapper. For the next eight years Davis was both the mentor and the father figure he never had in his own stolid parent. A bachelor, Bob Davis was in his fifties when he and young Dwight Eisenhower became fast friends. In Eisenhower the older man had a willing pupil who was eager to absorb his knowledge. Davis imbued Eisenhower with his knowledge of fishing, trapping, poling a flatboat with a single oar, duck shooting, and how to cook over a campfire. Besides a teacher and an inspiration, Eisenhower exuberantly found in Bob Davis a living link to the glory days of Abilene. It was no coincidence that Dwight Eisenhower was considered the best shot in the family. While in high school he inherited a 16-gauge, pump-action Winchester shotgun from older brother Edgar, with which he hunted wolves, coyotes, and jackrabbits. So great was his love of hunting that he organized hunting trips to a favorite retreat twenty miles south of Abilene, called Lyon's Creek. Thanks to his growing prowess as a cook, no one went hungry.[9]

Bob Davis's most enduring legacy is undoubtedly what he taught Dwight Eisenhower about the game of poker. Although illiterate, Davis showed Eisenhower how to play poker successfully, if conservatively. During camping trips Davis drilled into Eisenhower a card sense based on percentages and odds. With his natural skill at mathematics and the lessons imparted by the worldly Davis, Eisenhower eventually developed into a master player who years later would supplement his meager army pay at the poker table. There were few secrets in the Eisenhower household, but Dwight's poker education was one that he kept to himself.[10]

. . .

When the Eisenhowers moved from Denison, Texas, to Abilene in 1892, the town was still primitive, with no sewers, no paved roads (until 1910), and a water supply that served only the elite north side. The sidewalks were wood planks, and stones were placed at street corners to facilitate crossings in bad weather. A mule-drawn streetcar line provided transportation. Milk was available only from those owning cows or from street peddlers, who sold it from open containers. The fire department used horse-drawn equipment until 1915, and its volunteer firemen were summoned by means of a loud whistle at the Belle Springs Creamery. There was a one-man (later two) police force, whose chief function was to collect "the [annual] two-dollar poll tax levied on all adult males and chasing truant youngsters" and to check that the local merchants had locked their doors.[11] The adult citizens of Abilene were all frontier pioneers who had brought with them the virtues of plain speaking, their strong religious beliefs, and a trust that hard work and success went hand in hand.

Strong social divisions prevailed in Abilene between the haves and the have-nots. The dividing line was the Union Pacific railroad tracks, which bisected the town. The contrast between the two was obvious: To the north were the fine Victorian homes of the well-to-do situated along affluent Buckeye and Third Streets; to the south working-class families like the Eisenhowers resided in smaller wood-frame houses. Many lived well below the poverty line. The religious and social life of the town was centered in Abilene's numerous churches, where its citizens came together to pray and to partake in group picnics. One of the many carnivals of that era was based in Abilene. The carnival families all lived in Abilene's south side, and their children attended elementary school with the Eisenhowers. Ike's boyhood friend John E. Long remembered "an unusual number of bad boys," who offered ample opportunities for fighting—of which Dwight Eisenhower took his fair share.[12]

David Eisenhower went to work at the Belle Springs Creamery as a maintenance engineer in March 1892. By the early 1900s the business would grow to become one of the largest and most successful independent creameries in the entire Midwest.[13] The creamery account book for 1892 reveals that on March 12, the owner, a member of the River Brethren named J. E. Nissley, hired D. J. Eisenhower at an annual salary of $350.[14] The title "engineer" was a euphemism. His work at the creamery involved twelve-hour days and hard manual labor maintaining the machinery and steam equipment. It wasn't much, but Eisenhower never complained: The family's obvious delight at being back in the company of family and friends outweighed the paucity of David's salary and the humble nature of his work. Even so, the family thrived through its own self-sufficiency. Except for a break in service due to illness in 1912, David Eisenhower worked for the Belle Springs Creamery for twenty-four years, before leaving in 1916 for a similar position at the local gas plant, where he was soon promoted to general manager, a position he held until his retirement in 1931. During his thirty-nine years of toil in Abilene David Eisenhower never earned more than $150 per month.[15]

Dwight Eisenhower's first and perhaps most lasting recollection of his childhood occurred shortly before his fifth birthday, when his aunt escorted him by rail, then by horse and buggy, to a family gathering on a farm near Topeka, where most of Ida's relatives resided. His recollections were typical of what children experience when thrust into a strange environment for the first time. "It was peculiar to be surrounded by so many strangers. It seemed to me that there were dozens or hundreds of people—all grown-ups—in the house. Even though they were, somehow, my family, I felt lonesome and lost among them."[16]

Eisenhower fled the house for the sanctuary of the barnyard, which he began exploring until he encountered a particularly bad-tempered, aggressive male goose that deemed the youngster's presence a territorial affront. Frightened but determined not to be intimidated by this surly creature, Eisenhower wept tears of frustration after he was repeatedly driven from the barnyard. Taking pity, his uncle Luther (Stover) stripped an old broom of its straw, showed the child how to employ it as a weapon, and then left him to fend for himself. More afraid of the disapprobation of his uncle and his relatives than of the surly goose, a trembling Eisenhower advanced, yelling, and gave the goose "a satisfying smack on the fanny." Though still belligerent, the goose never again bothered Eisenhower. The self-esteem of a five-year-old boy was restored and, more important, the lesson imparted in his uncle's farmyard that day was not lost on young Eisenhower, who later recalled: "I learned never to negotiate with an adversary except from a position of strength."[17]

Eisenhower's favorite relative was his vibrant Uncle Abe, who found his true calling as an itinerant preacher. Part preacher, part carnival barker, and part happy-go-lucky gypsy, Abe traveled into western Kansas and the Oklahoma territory in a large, unwieldy, covered, horse-drawn vehicle he nicknamed the "gospel wagon." Abe knew how to attract a crowd of strangers with cries of "This way to heaven!," then mesmerize them with rousing sermons. In 1901, Abe and his wife founded a missionary home for orphans in Guthrie, Oklahoma, before eventually moving to California. Years later, when Abe's nephew had become world famous, Dwight Eisenhower would tell friends that he was "damned if I've ever been able to figure out" the message of his uncle's sermons. "I know the old man was mighty proud of himself, the way he could raise an audience out of dust."[18]

When Abe left Abilene in 1898, David and Ida were given possession of his house, located a few blocks away at 201 Southeast Fourth Street. Situated on three acres of land that included a large barn, the two-story white frame home was surrounded by maple trees and seemed like a mansion after six years in the tiny, cramped house on Second Street. It can only be imagined what David and Ida's reaction might have been had they known that their permanent home (now the location of the Eisenhower Center) once adjoined the site of the wild and wicked whorehouses of the "Devil's Addition" during Abilene's heyday.[19]

Still, with eight people living in it, the Eisenhowers' new home was hardly spacious. The rooms were small by modern standards. Daily life revolved around organization, cooperation, and a vast array of duties, alternated weekly among the brothers, from which no one was exempt. Merely feeding six growing boys with enormous appetites was itself an exceptional logistical feat. As brother Earl remembers, "That house was all things to us, football field, boxing arena, chapel, assembly line, study room, emergency hospital, cooking school and hobby center. It was, in short, 'home,' a good place for boys to grow into men."[20]

Dwight's first household duties consisted of collecting kindling for the stove and shaving it into pieces. Often he would start bawling to attract attention, in the vain hope that parental sympathy would relieve him of this chore. "I was a great bawler when I was very young . . . I remember a neighbor lady coming in one day and saying, 'Ida, what are you doing to that child?' She said, 'Oh, he'll be all right as soon as he brings his kindling in.' And, of course, I was."[21] Attempts at intimidation never worked either. Edgar once threatened to run away from home. His father suggested various routes he might take, while his mother offered to prepare a lunch for him to take along.

In summer each son tended his own garden plot in addition to working in the nearby cornfield and the rest of the family plot. Dwight became an adept gardener and a shrewd young businessman who grew and peddled the vegetables most in demand, usually cucumbers and sweet corn. David permitted his sons to earn their own spending money. Dwight's usually went to purchase athletic equipment. In his memoirs Eisenhower recounts the valuable lessons he learned about money.[22] The many duties performed by the Eisenhower boys were part of Ida's domain and included cooking; dishwashing; laundry; milking the family cow; feeding the chickens; putting hay in their large barn; weeding, pruning, and maintaining the gardens and cornfield; and harvesting and storing the fruit. Their large garden was so carefully cultivated that it yielded an abundance of fruit and vegetables. Rounding out the family menagerie were two cows, numerous chickens, several pigs, and Belgian hares. During the growing season, the only chores universally despised were those inside the house. "To help meet household expenses," remembered Edgar, "mother often sent Dwight and me over to the north side of town with our little red wagon loaded with sweet corn, peas, beans, tomatoes and eggs." Although it never visibly bothered Dwight, Edgar never got over his deep resentment at the haughtiness of some of their snooty customers, who he sensed regarded them as little better than panhandlers.[23]

The most odious chores of all were cleaning out the chicken coop and washing the family clothes, a complicated process involving copious gallons of water that had to be boiled to heat the washing machine. Washing the smelly diapers of the youngest Eisenhowers was a duty no one wanted.

Another duty performed by the older boys was to take turns pushing Milton or Earl in a baby buggy. Either through lethargy or perhaps a determination to do things his own way, Dwight would lie on the floor or, if outside, on the grass, and with his feet or a rope tied to the buggy, push it back and forth to the complete satisfaction of its occupant. It also became a means of indulging his passion for reading while ostensibly performing a family duty. For a time Dwight was also responsible for putting Earl to bed at night and dressing him in the morning, a task he despised.[24]

The Eisenhower boys also shared the cooking duties. When it was their turn on a Sunday, Dwight and Edgar returned home after Sunday school at the nearby River Brethren church to prepare dinner while the rest of the family attended the service. On one occasion the two decided it would be fun to make a pie. They rolled up the dough and began playing catch with it. Although the dough was dropped on the floor several times, the brothers baked a somewhat discolored but nevertheless delicious pie. As with everything he ever took seriously, Eisenhower worked assiduously to become a first-class cook, which, his high jinks aside, became a valuable skill that would prove immensely useful in the years ahead.[25]

The main staple of the family diet was potatoes, which were served at virtually every meal. The prodigious amounts of potatoes consumed by the Eisenhower boys eventually spawned a ditty they repeated:

> Oh, the 'taters they grew small,
> And we ate them skin and all,
> Out in Kansas. . . . [26]

For the rest of his life Dwight Eisenhower viewed everything through the prism of the "waste not, want not" virtue instilled in him as a youth. He thought any excess deplorable, and once at a banquet in Chicago after World War II, Chris Musser claims to have seen him cut a large steak in half and send the other half back to the kitchen with a pronouncement that as long as people were starving elsewhere in the world, food should not be wasted.[27]

The family had no alarm clock, nor did they need one. "Dad was the alarm clock," and at 5:30 A.M. he would come to the bottom of the stairs and call out, "Boys!," which was their signal to begin a new day. Dwight was the hardest of the sons to awaken and often had to be cajoled or threatened from his bed. During cold weather they dressed under the covers; in summer the house became nearly unbearable, with the heat often exceeding one hundred degrees.

For many years there was neither running water nor indoor plumbing. In the bitter cold of winter, when temperatures often dropped below zero, a trip to the outhouse was an adventure not soon forgotten. Except in summer, when the water was heated outside by the sun, bathing involved filling a large tub in the kitchen using water heated on the stove. Usually the bathwater was used by more than one boy, and since bathing was on a first-come basis there was always intense competition to be the first. For many years none of the boys even knew what a bathtub was.[28]

It was a rule in the Eisenhower household that no one was permitted to leave the dinner table until after Ida said, "Amen." Dwight usually sat on a stool, champing at the bit to be freed of this symbol of family togetherness. His anxiety was evident by his habit of stealthily turning on the stool to face outward, as if to obtain a head start. When his mother finally pronounced the magic word, "he was off and gone like a shot." For a time Ida even worried that her impetuous young son somehow might not turn out very well.[29]

A significant part of their lives revolved around baseball and football. The boys lost no opportunity to play their favorite games, even in the kitchen where Dwight would wash plates, then throw them to Ed on first base, who tossed them to Art or Milton covering home. It is a tribute to their athletic skills that there were no broken dishes, which would surely have ended their kitchen sport.[30]

David Eisenhower's exile in Texas had failed to mellow his enmity toward Milton Good. During their youth the Eisenhower sons all learned David's version of the affair. No bill could ever be carried over, even if it meant the family had to do without.[31] Dwight Eisenhower and his brothers were left with an enduring and bitter conviction that their father had been grievously wronged by Milton Good.[32]

Although it had been 150 years since the first Eisenhower had arrived in America, German was still the mother tongue of his Abilene descendants. Jacob's years of generosity to his family had left him financially strapped in his old age, and in the final years before his death he lived with David and Ida. David and Jacob conversed almost exclusively in German, but with Jacob's death in 1906, the custom ended. Thereafter David refused to speak German to Ida or his sons, in the belief that they were better off being like other children in Abilene who spoke only English.[33]

Once settled in Abilene, the Eisenhower family continued to grow at a rapid rate. As each new birth took place, David and Ida's yearning for a girl was again dashed. Roy was born in 1892, followed by Paul in 1894. Almost nothing is known of baby Paul, who was apparently sickly from birth and was only ten months old at the time of his death from diphtheria in 1895.

David and Ida managed to keep their deeply felt grief private and thus never conveyed a lasting impression to any of their six surviving sons.

The Eisenhowers had no more children until 1898, when Earl was born. The baby brother of the family, Milton, arrived in 1899. By now the parents, particularly David, openly longed for a baby girl and were sorely disappointed at the birth of yet another son.[34]

Arthur, Roy, and Milton were dark-haired and resembled their father, but, like his mother, Dwight's eyes were blue and his hair was so light blond that he was often referred to as "Swede." Earl, whose reddish-blond hair made him a genetic throwback to his grandfather, lost the sight in his left eye from a tragic mishap at the age of four that would obsess Dwight Eisenhower for the rest of his life. The incident took place in the family toolshed, where Dwight was busily making a toy while Earl played nearby. A butcher knife he had just used was carefully placed on a nearby windowsill to keep it away from his brother. Dwight failed to notice that the inquisitive Earl had managed to climb on a chair, where he attempted to grasp the knife, which fell and struck him in the left eye. Earl's eye was permanently damaged, and several years later he lost his sight in the eye entirely while roughhousing with Milton. At Ida's insistence that no one should be blamed, the accident was never again spoken of by the Eisenhowers. Although Ida was attempting to instill in her sons the notion that life is risky and that while accidents happen, lingering resentments were self-destructive, her admonition had the opposite effect on Dwight, who was remorseful for the remainder of his life.[35]

More than any of the other Eisenhower sons, Dwight inherited his father's violent temper. Examples of his rages as a child are legendary. The Eisenhower brothers fought frequently, often with bloody results. Dwight, Edgar, and Earl had the hottest tempers, but it was Edgar and Dwight who had the greatest rivalry and the most fights. "You were always vastly my superior," Dwight acknowledged in 1944. "You could run faster, hit better, field better, tote the foot-ball better, and do everything except beat me at shotgun shooting. . . . I was just the tail to your kite."[36] None of which deterred Dwight from continually taking on Edgar in frustration and an unfulfilled determination to best his older brother. Whether it was sporting competition, who had first rights to the *Saturday Evening Post*, or for the most trivial reason, rivalries abounded in the Eisenhower household. Nevertheless Dwight's son, John Sheldon Doud Eisenhower, is justifiably suspicious that their claims of combat were grossly exaggerated. "I doubt that anyone could fight as much as they say they did," he has said, noting that the tale of Dwight losing a wrestling match with his father "probably lost nothing in the telling."[37] Still, Eisenhower's steely resolve, whether in coping with the responsibilities of high command or staring down Russian premier Nikita Khrushchev was a reflection of the lessons learned at the hands of a stern, uncompromising father.[38]

"Hate" was a nonexistent word in the Eisenhower family vocabulary, but David and his son Dwight both possessed long memories for those unfortunate enough to have aroused their anger. David so rarely spoke that he left the perception that inside the man lay a heart of darkness rarely lit. Even his own sons believed that he was far too solemn, and there is no known photograph in which David Eisenhower is seen to be smiling. Certainly he contributed little to prepare his sons for adulthood and "managed to be absent even when he was present." His life revolved around his work. "He never came home for lunch . . . reappeared at six in the evening, to say grace at the start of supper, eat silently through it, then hole up in a room with a book."[39]

A forceful example of both Dwight Eisenhower's sense of family and his explosive temper was expressed in 1947 on the occasion of a visit to Abilene. When he found that a sign had been erected in front of the family home announcing that it was the boyhood home of General Eisenhower, his face flushed red and his famous temper erupted: "That sign is not right. This is the boyhood home of the Eisenhower family. I want it changed immediately." The next day it was.[40]

The most important lesson the Eisenhowers taught their sons was that they must think and shift for themselves. Edgar notes: "There was bred into us a certain independence and a determination to rise above our humble beginnings and try to some day amount to something."[41] It became an absolute article of faith in the minds of their sons that being poor was no disgrace and no less honorable than being born rich. What counted was one's faith and old-fashioned hard work.

David and Ida's sons had no inclination to disparage their poverty. They were always neatly dressed in clean clothes handed down from one brother to the next. Clothes and shoes were altered, mended, and—however threadbare—eventually passed down the family ladder to the youngest sons, Earl and Milton. Nothing was ever wasted. Having their own shoes was prized, but during warm weather the boys often attended school barefoot. Mending became such a burdensome task that Ida taught each of the boys how to darn his own socks. The result was that they developed a healthy respect for the value of money and possessions.[42]

Nevertheless, memories of Dwight Eisenhower's childhood poverty still clung, even in his old age. On one occasion after his second presidential term, he and Mamie visited a clothing store in Ayr, Scotland. Eisenhower's eyes lit up at the sight of such fine clothing. The clerk who made a large sale to the Eisenhowers was overheard to opine that the former president "acted like a lad from the hills," which Eisenhower thought "may well be one of the better compliments paid me in recent years." He also recalled that the compliment he received from the Scottish clerk would never have happened in Abilene. When it came to forking over money, "the canny Scots of Ayr could not hold a candle to us in our painstakingly critical scrutiny of goods and prices. . . .

The Indian on our penny would have screamed if we could have possibly have held it tighter."[43]

The Eisenhower family's return to stability in Abilene also brought about a change in David and Ida's approach to religion. The six Eisenhower brothers all attended the River Brethren Sunday school, where Dwight and his brothers "never seemed to pay any attention or take any interest in the lesson."[44] Although the River Brethren were still the centerpiece of their spiritual lives, David and Ida began searching for new meanings and became interested in a fundamentalist sect then known as the Bible Students.[45] According to Edgar, "The meetings were held at our house, and everyone made his own interpretation of the Scripture lessons. Mother played the piano, and they sang hymns before and after each meeting. . . . They talked to God, read Scriptures, and everyone got a chance to state his relationship with Him. . . . I have never forgotten those Scripture lessons, nor the influence they have had on my life. Simple people taking a simple approach to God. We couldn't have forgotten because mother impressed those creeds deep in our memories."[46] During the services Dwight and his brothers were permitted to remain outside, where they played such games as blindman's bluff and hide-and-seek.

When the River Brethren failed to provide the solace they sought in the wake of baby Paul's death in 1895, Ida became a convert to the Bible Student movement, which in 1931 adopted the name "Jehovah's Witnesses." David is thought to have involved himself reluctantly to placate Ida until about 1915, when he ceased any religious involvement.

Those closest to the Eisenhower family remember it as a happy house, free of friction. And Milton recalled of his parents, "I never heard a cross word pass between them."[47] The sons not only listened to David and Ida read the Bible during a daily ritual but were often permitted to read from it themselves. Bible readings were deemed an honor, but there was one explicit house rule: The privilege ended whenever the reader made a mistake and was caught by another of the boys. Eisenhower believed that these family Bible readings greatly simplified the requirement to read aloud in front of his teachers and classmates.

By the age of twelve Eisenhower had read the entire Bible, and by the time he left Abilene in 1911, he had read it for a second time. He remembered most of what he read, and during World War II would frequently astonish his aides by his ability to quote from memory a suitable passage for any occasion.

Until the time of his presidency, Dwight Eisenhower never attended church, and, as adults, none of the Eisenhower sons followed the religious beliefs of their parents, but all were deeply affected by their religious upbringing. "Clearly the dominant religious influence in the Eisenhower home from the time the boys were young was Watchtower theology and beliefs."[48] Nevertheless their mother's religious affiliation appears to have been a source of considerable embarrassment. Ida had subscribed to the official Witnesses' publication, the *Watchtower*, but after her death in 1946, Milton quietly disposed of his mother's fifty-year-old collection lest there be undue publicity. Although Dwight briefly acknowledged his mother's association with the Witnesses in his memoir, his brothers rarely spoke of Ida's religious beliefs and then only in vague terms. Milton, in particular, would concede only that "we were raised as a fundamentalist family."[49] Throughout his life, Dwight Eisenhower would reaffirm his religious upbringing in various ways. During World War II it was often simply to ask for "God's guidance in making the right decision."[50] Ida was fond of playing solitaire, and from this pastime emerged one of her many homilies that became a guiding principle of his life: "The Lord deals the cards; you play them."[51]

In 1906 Jacob Eisenhower died at the age of eighty after a long and successful life. As a child, Dwight remembered him for his black dress, his underbeard, and particularly for his horse and buggy, riding in which became a sought-after luxury. Only as an adult would Eisenhower fully recognize the unique qualities of his pioneer-farmer grandfather. His worth "rests far more on his own deeds, on the family he raised and the spiritual heritage he left them, than on one grandson," he wrote.[52]

Ida was understanding and tolerant, but there were occasions when Dwight exceeded her dictum: "He who conquers his temper is greater than he who taketh the city."[53] Although she was not above slapping an errant hand, the real discipline fell to David, whose explosive temper was on full display the day Edgar was severely whipped for having quit school without permission to earn money working for a local doctor. Dwight was twelve years old and witnessed Edgar being severely beaten with a leather harness and began shouting at his father to stop. Ignored, he began to cry, partly in the hope his mother would come to the rescue. When he attempted to grab his father's arms only to be asked if he wanted some of the same, Dwight hotly replied, "I don't think anyone ought to be whipped like that, not even a dog." Both brothers rationalized their father's rage as a severe but necessary means of teaching Edgar not to jeopardize his future.[54] On other disciplinary occasions, as often as not, the recipient was the rebellious young Dwight Eisenhower.

Dwight credits his mother with teaching him to control his temper. One Halloween when he was about ten years old, his two older brothers were given permission to venture out with a group of local youths. Dwight was deemed too young and became so agitated that, in a blind rage, he began beating the apple tree in front of the house with his fists. "For some reason, I guess, I thought the apple tree was to blame and I was there crying as hard as I could and beating this apple tree with my fists, and they were all bleeding and messy."[55] His tantrum earned Dwight a severe thrashing from his father, who ordered him to his bed.

A short time later Ida arrived with a washcloth and salve to clean and wrap Dwight's bleeding hands. Using some Bible verses by way of explanation, she calmly demonstrated to her mercurial son why he was only harming himself by such irrational displays of behavior. "I think that was one of the most important moments of my life," recalled Eisenhower, "because since then . . . I've gotten angry many times, but I certainly have tried to keep from showing it."[56] Nevertheless Eisenhower never fully gained control of his temper.

The Eisenhower sons recognized David's contributions to their upbringing, but they were in awe of Ida, the glue that held the family together during the good times and the bad. Her influence upon her sons was incalculable, none more so than on Dwight Eisenhower, who venerated her. Throughout World War II, when the heavy responsibility of the Western Alliance rested on his shoulders, Eisenhower thought often and fondly of Ida, wishing that somehow he could see her and be calmed and reassured by her presence and her wisdom. "I think my mother is the finest person I've ever known," he wrote in a note to himself in March 1942.[57] No wonder Eisenhower would later say of his beloved mother, "For her sons, privileged to spend a boyhood in her company, the memories are indelible. . . . Mother was by far the greatest personal influence on our lives."[58]

Her niece, Nettie Stover Jackson, recalled how Ida once said, "I studied each of my boys to know how to deal with them," each as a unique individual, and to respond accordingly.[59] She urged them to behave not out of fear of the consequences of disobedience but "because it was the right thing to do."[60] To her death, she treated all her sons as equals. When a reporter once asked Ida what she thought of her most famous son, she replied, "Which son do you mean?"[61]

Each of the Eisenhower sons had a distinctive character. As the eldest, Arthur accepted the role with equanimity and little fanfare. Although quick tempered like all the Eisenhower brothers, Arthur is remembered by Dwight as the son who gave his parents the least trouble and was the best behaved. Unlike the others Arthur cared little for either athletics or fisticuffs, although he indulged in his fair share of the latter when provoked. Starting at the bottom of the ladder, Arthur became a successful banker in Kansas City.

Edgar matched Dwight's fiery temperament in every way. A man of boundless energy and intemperate and impulsive behavior, Edgar was the most sentimental of the brothers, a trait unshared by Dwight. Financially Edgar was the most successful of the Eisenhowers, but although he became a millionaire, he too never forgot the privations of his childhood. His reputation as one of the south side's toughest youths was well earned, but his energy as a grown man was channeled into a successful and highly lucrative law practice in Tacoma, Washington, while his famous brother lived much more modestly for most of his life.

Dwight never bested Edgar, but their lifelong sibling rivalry left him determined eventually to prevail over his older brother. His "don't get mad, get even" attitude carried over into his West Point years, and in 1913 Eisenhower challenged his brother, then a law student at the University of Michigan, to any competition he would accept, whether boxing, wrestling, or bare knuckles. A far more mature Edgar politely declined, but even in his old age Dwight remembered being "robbed of sweet revenge."[62] As their paths crossed less and less as grown men, the closeness they once shared seemed to wane, leaving in its place some lingering resentments from childhood, at least on Dwight's part. Whenever the subject of his youthful rivalry with Dwight arose, Edgar, even at the age of sixty-six, would assert, "I still can lick him anytime."[63] The rivalry and occasional bad feeling between Dwight and Edgar ended only with their respective deaths.

Roy became a pharmacist in nearby Junction City and seems to have had the clearest vision of his future profession. Some thought Roy most resembled his father, but he lacked David's brooding nature, was unpretentious and full of life, and loved sports and a good joke. He was perhaps the most social of the six brothers. Dwight, however, thought him "a bit of a lone wolf."[64]

The least known was Earl, a modest man who shunned the limelight in his chosen field as an electrical engineer for a utility company in Pennsylvania. Later he changed professions and became the general manager of a biweekly rural newspaper in Illinois. Earl preferred small-town life and possessed the distinction of being the only Eisenhower son to escape the curse of baldness.

To compensate for his physical ailments as a child, Dwight's kid brother, Milton, became the family scholar and a gifted educator and statesman. The eight-year age difference between Dwight and Milton was significant when they were children, but as grown men the two would eventually bond with an intimacy that did not exist between any of the other brothers.

Dwight was the most volatile and perhaps the most stubborn of David and Ida's sons. He was too young to compete with his two older brothers in sports or fighting, and too old to connect in a meaningful way with his younger brothers.

The one distinction that all six brothers had in common was their burning desire to obtain a one-way ticket out of Abilene in order to escape the fate that had befallen their father. Although Abilene has become legendary for its connection to the Eisenhowers, the sons of David and Ida Eisenhower fully understood that their respective destinies lay elsewhere. "They were all good guys," remembers John. "The six brothers were very different in many ways, but they were alike in all being driven men . . . they saw a highly educated, intelligent father live his life in near poverty and frustration and each concluded, 'This isn't going to happen to me.' "[65]

However, the long-perpetuated notion that the Eisenhower sons never knew they were poor is part of the myth created as early as 1942, when the print media hastened to investigate and publicize in the most heroic manner this heretofore unknown American and his family. To the contrary, their poverty was unavoidably obvious to each of the Eisenhower sons. Their fights, said John Eisenhower, "stemmed from the fact that, though Dwight Eisenhower claimed that the Eisenhowers never knew they were poor, they were definitely from the wrong side of the tracks (literally). But they were proud, and that fact brought on combats with the snobbish elements in town."[66] Biographer Peter Lyon accurately notes, "There is no question that poverty steeled young Dwight's ambition and his determination to excel, to succeed."[67]

For the most part, horseplay and fighting were a harmless means of letting off excess energy. Although their parents disapproved of fighting or even any form of quarreling, Dwight learned to his surprise that there were times when it was justified in his father's eyes. One day, for example, David returned home just as Dwight was being chased into their front yard by another child. When his father inquired why he tolerated being pushed around, Dwight replied, "Because if I fight him, you'll give me a whipping, whether I win or lose!" Instead David ordered him to chase the fellow away, and his son responded by throwing his tormentor to the ground and, although it was mostly bluff, "voiced threats of violence." The incident taught another childhood lesson that Eisenhower never forgot, namely that to feign domination of others is often just as effective as physical force.[68] Ida generally turned a blind eye to her sons' altercations, and when Dwight once came home with his face swollen, she merely asked if it had been a fair fight.

In May 1903 Kansas was ravaged by the worst flood in the state's history. In Abilene, both Mud Creek and the Smoky Hill River flooded south Abilene. Edgar and Dwight treated the disaster as a marvelous opportunity for a great adventure. The two decided it would be exciting to ride the floodwaters down Buckeye Street, on a broken piece of wooden sidewalk that made a serviceable raft upon which they imagined themselves as pirates, loudly singing "Marching Through Georgia." Their merriment left both oblivious to the fact that they were in danger of being swept into the raging Smoky Hill River and drowning. The soaking-wet boys were jarred from their reverie by a man on horseback who sternly ordered them to return to Abilene through waters that by then were waist high. Only then did it dawn on the two adventurers that they had completely forgotten their only reason for being outside that day—to deliver their father's lunch to the creamery. For once an irate Ida did not spare the rod. Still bemused many years later, Edgar recalled that "the thrashing taught us a most important rule of boyhood; namely, don't forget your father's lunch."[69]

4.

A Young Man's Education

My hand was made less for the use of the pen than of the ax—or possibly a pistol.

Eisenhower entered Lincoln Elementary School in 1896 at the age of six. Virtually all who enter the alien world of primary school for the first time have vivid, often unwelcome memories of the occasion. Although used to a regimented existence at home, Eisenhower well remembered that day as a cataclysmic experience.[1] Situated near the family home on Abilene's south side, the school lacked lighting or indoor plumbing and was dark and forbidding in winter. For the first few years, slates were used for writing, with paper furnished only from about the sixth grade. Learning was by the traditional method of repetition and offered little incentive to hold a child's interest. Eisenhower's boredom was only assuaged by an infrequent spelling bee or the "suppression of a disorderly boy."

Although education in Eisenhower's time was intended to produce informed citizens, there was little endorsement in places like Abilene for education unless it had some demonstrably practical value. As Eisenhower notes, "It was a male-run society and schools were preponderately feminine," by about two to one.[2] A college education was simply a fantasy for most at a time when few young people even completed high school. Of the two hundred students who entered the first grade at Abilene's two elementary schools in 1897, a mere sixty-seven entered the town's high school.

Although dismal and unrewarding, school was not all work. Recess was a time to let off steam as only young boys can. Their usual recreation was a game called shinny, a "ground version of ice hockey with rules made up on the spot and promptly ignored. They used sticks or whatever they could find for clubs and the puck was a battered tin can. Dwight excelled at this dangerous game and could always be found where the action was the roughest." A corner of the school grounds overlooked his future home, then Uncle Abe's house. One of their favorite pastimes was to line up and watch him treat animals on an improvised table and sling in the yard until the clanging of a triangle signaled the end of recess.[3]

Eisenhower's favorite subjects in grammar school were spelling and arithmetic, which to his logical mind meant that there was never any ambiguity whatsoever in what one did. His interest in proper usage of words turned into a near obsession, and their misapplication he deemed inexcusable. The pragmatic side of Eisenhower can be seen in his love of mathematics. "Practical problems have always been my equivalent of crossword puzzles."[4] Although he practiced it regularly, Eisenhower's penmanship was dreadful, and he never bothered to learn the elaborate Victorian style of the times. "My hand was made less for the use of the pen than of the ax—or possibly a pistol," he later said.[5] Deciphering Eisenhower's handwriting was invariably a challenge to others but never more so than after he became a general. Eisenhower himself could not always read his own writing, which was as contorted as his father's had been neat and elegant. Kevin McCann, a postwar assistant, likened it to something that was written on a lazy Susan, while his longtime friend and military colleague, Gen. Alfred Gruenther, described it as among the world's worst. A junior high school classmate, Wilbur Jeffcoat, laughingly recalled, "I never became president but I sure as heck can write legibly and Eisenhower can't."[6]

Fight as they might among themselves, the brothers would not tolerate others picking on one of their own. To the contrary, Eisenhower seemed to relish confronting a bully or someone clearly superior in size.[7] In 1902 Eisenhower moved to Garfield Junior High School, where he spent the seventh and eighth grades. Situated on the town's north side, Garfield was a mix of students from both north and south. During recess on Dwight's first day, a much bigger bully chased him around the playground threatening to bite off his ears until Arthur intervened and warned the boy to "have your fun with someone else." Although he later realized it was mostly teasing, until he grew strong enough to fend for himself, young Eisenhower was terrified of bullies and their threats. When that day came he never again backed down from the challenge of another or shied from a fight. One day Eisenhower tackled and subdued a particularly large and unpleasant tormentor who was wielding a dangerous weapon in the form of a large steel nut attached to a cord, daring anyone to touch him. As classmate John Long recalled, "From that time on whenever there was any kind of trouble on the school grounds [the students] always wailed 'Ike, Ike, Ike,' " even if he was not involved.[8]

Dwight and his brothers eventually acquired a well-earned reputation as "those little roughnecks from the wrong side of the railroad tracks."[9] By the time they were enrolled in Garfield, both Edgar and Dwight were regarded as the best bare-knuckle fighters in the tough south side. Long before the word "macho" was ever coined, the young men of Abilene, like the Eisenhowers, could lay claim to having acted out the continuing fantasy of the bad old days when it was a Wild West cowtown. Every year there were one or more significant scraps between the two sides for pride and bragging rights during the school term. "We didn't go around looking for them," said Edgar. "No one knew in advance who the combatants would be. They just happened."[10] A large crowd of spectators would form a circle around the fighters in a vacant lot, and only the winner would walk away. That an Eisenhower would be involved was virtually inevitable, and with Dwight now attending Garfield, it came as no surprise that he would be obliged to uphold what had become something of an Eisenhower tradition, as well as the honor of the south siders.

The most wildly exaggerated tale of Eisenhower's boyhood was his alleged marathon fight with a tough north sider named Wesley Merrifield in October 1903. The year before, Edgar had beaten a larger opponent senseless to claim the honor of south side superiority. Dwight was just thirteen when he was obliged to fight Merrifield in a nearby vacant lot in the presence of a large crowd. Neither boy had any inclination to fight the other, particularly for the amusement of a howling mob. Both, however, were eventually intimidated by irresistible pressure from classmates. "The two of us were practically forced together. Neither of us had the courage to say, 'I won't fight,' " wrote Eisenhower.[11] This much is true.

Abilene lore has it that Eisenhower was given no chance against the stronger, faster, bull-like Merrifield. The first full account of the battle was written by Kenneth Davis and has been widely repeated and exploited to turn a fairly ordinary schoolboy fight into a heroic two-hour test of endurance in which Eisenhower is said to have fearlessly withstood the challenge of a bully. The reality was that there was far more pushing and shoving than fisticuffs. In his memoir, Eisenhower recalled that the two went at each other for about an hour, "with occasional pauses for breath."[12]

Whether the fight lasted twenty minutes or an hour, it was said to have ended in a draw when both became too exhausted to continue. Eisenhower later quoted Merrifield saying, " 'I can't lick you.' I said the same thing, and that was that." Eisenhower sustained a black eye that was too obvious to hide from his parents, who kept him out of school for several days. "I got off with a strong reprimand," he recalled.[13] He had long since proved his resilience and physical courage, but a decade later he willingly conceded that Merrifield had licked him. Other than enhancing Eisenhower's reputation in the Abilene community, the most notable aspect of the fight was that Merrifield would be remembered for having fought a future five-star general and president of the United States.

In the autumn of 1904 Eisenhower entered Abilene High School, which was then situated in makeshift quarters on the second floor of the city hall. One room served as the chapel, and the teachers took turns leading devotional services and giving lectures on the Bible and its various Scriptures.[14] The city jail and the quarters of the town fire marshal occupied the first floor. The male students served in the Abilene volunteer fire department. The town fire bell was situated in a cupola in one of the recitation rooms, and whenever it rang to summon them to a fire, Eisenhower and his classmates would seize the opportunity to skip school by helping out. A friend and classmate, Lelia Picking, recalls, "If Dwight didn't get to the hose cart he was among those who sprinted to the store to buy treats for the girls." One morning the students arrived to find that a prisoner had dynamited a corner of the building during an attempted jailbreak, leading one teacher later to observe wryly that the students received their education "midst the howling of the dogs, the wailing of the prisoners and the odor of the onions being cooked for the marshal's dinner."[15]

In the spring of 1905, when Eisenhower was fourteen and in his first year at Abilene High School, what began as a seemingly minor knee abrasion after a fall led to the creation of another exaggerated tale of Dwight Eisenhower's youth. It was a story of near death and miraculous recovery told within the family and related melodramatically to Eisenhower's first biographer, Kenneth Davis—and subsequently repeated in other biographies. What is certain is that the wound became infected, and after several days, Eisenhower's left knee became swollen and quite painful. Fearing the worst when she noticed a black streak running up his thigh, Ida immediately summoned the Eisenhower family physician, Dr. Tracy R. Conklin, known familiarly as "Doc Conklin," who was well respected throughout the Abilene community.

According to the tale, Conklin is thought to have confirmed Ida's worst fear: that Dwight was in an advanced stage of blood poisoning, and if it infected his abdomen, he would die. Dwight's fever was said to have risen so high that he had sunk into a semicoma. Conklin repeatedly urged the Eisenhowers to permit him to amputate Dwight's poisoned leg in order to save his life. Terrified that if he lost his leg he would never again play sports, Eisenhower supposedly declared he'd rather die. Edgar claimed his younger brother extracted a promise that Conklin would not be permitted to take his leg. In his autobiography Edgar insists that he stationed himself in front of the bedroom door and warned, "Nobody's going to touch Dwight. . . . For two days I kept watch," permitting the doctor to enter the room only to medicate and bandage his brother's leg. A frustrated and helpless Conklin allegedly told the parents it was murder.[16] After some three days, however, the fever miraculously abated and the ominous black line gradually disappeared. That Dwight's life and his leg had been saved was viewed by the family as nothing less than God's will.

According to one of Eisenhower's presidential physicians, who made an extensive study of his health, "it was labelled 'blood poisoning' at the time, but over the years physicians who have evaluated the characteristics of the infection have considered it to have been . . . a streptococcal infection of the skin and soft tissues."[17] Without antibiotics, which had yet to be discovered,

Eisenhower's wound could only have been healed by his immune system. What was thought to have been a coma was almost certainly delirium brought on by the high fever. That he was well conditioned and in the peak of health are the more probable reasons why Eisenhower did not die from the infection.[18] His recovery kept him out of school for the remainder of the school term, which obliged him to repeat his freshman year in 1905–06.[19]

Eisenhower later scoffed at the tales appearing in magazine and newspaper articles of how his distraught parents prayed continuously throughout his ordeal, but Edgar insists that there was indeed a great deal of prayer by everyone. "Doc Conklin admitted that he had once more met the medical man's superior—God Almighty."[20]

Conklin's granddaughter recalls that his wife was furious when Kenneth Davis's account was published in 1945. On more than one occasion she privately proclaimed that her husband's reputation had been besmirched by the Eisenhowers. "It was not the way things happened," she said, noting that her husband had never recommended amputating Dwight Eisenhower's leg.[21]

In 1907 a fine new high school opened farther uptown, finally bringing to an inglorious end the bizarre experiences Eisenhower and his classmates had had in the city hall. Although Edgar should have been several years ahead of Dwight in school, the year he skipped to work and an illness that kept him home for a year resulted in both attending Abilene High together.

During his early schooldays, he was called Dwight, but during his high school years, from 1905 to 1909, he was nicknamed "Little Ike," to distinguish him from Edgar, who was known as "Big Ike." Dwight was also sometimes called "Ugly Ike," an appellation whose origin was never clear. Ida heartily disapproved of the nickname "Ike" even though it was applied to all her sons at one time or another. When asked, she was likely to reply stubbornly, with a straight face, "Ike? Who's Ike?"[22]

Dwight is remembered as an extremely popular student who worked very hard at after-school jobs and thus had little time for socializing or involvement in any of the school clubs. His reputation was that of a tough, self-assured, and bright south-side youth who more than fulfilled his wish to be seen as one of the boys. The girls liked him for his seemingly carefree personality, and the boys appreciated his willingness to stand up to schoolyard bullies. However, girls were not high among Eisenhower's priorities, which began with sports, work, hunting, and even his studies. He was far more interested in impressing his peers with his athleticism or his fists. Other than close friendships with several girls from the south side, among them Ruby Norman, Gladys Harding, and Minnie Stewart, Eisenhower evinced little curiosity about the opposite sex and was shy in the company of young women, regarding himself as "gangly and awkward, with few of the social graces."[23] Once asked why he dated only rarely, Eisenhower replied that he had no money, no clothes, and no time. On the only occasion when he arranged a date with a north-side girl, she stood him up.[24] In reality, Eisenhower's purported indifference to the opposite sex masked an innate shyness that was usually manifested by his unkempt dress and disheveled hair. Nor did it enhance his self-confidence that, by his own admission, he was "a terrible dancer."[25]

He had yet to fall in love, although Ruby Norman, a pretty, vivacious redhead with violet eyes and a talent for the violin, appears to have had a serious crush on him. She was his first girlfriend, and the two dated now and then, usually taking in a film at the local movie house (which cost about five cents each), but mostly they were simply best friends. Eisenhower thought of Ruby as the sister he never had. Minnie Stewart was several years older and taught mathematics in the high school. She was in awe of Eisenhower and thought him "brilliant." Another girl he dated was Gladys Harding, whom he would later nearly marry.

Charles M. Harger, editor of the *Abilene Daily-Reflector* and one of Abilene's most respected citizens, knew Eisenhower well. "Coming to high school age, Dwight was a natural leader. He organized groups and was popular with teachers. He was no miracle child; he was just a strong, healthy boy with a serious mind, who looked upon the world as waiting for him—in what capacity he did not know. My daughter [Lois Bradshaw Harger] was in his class, and when a troop of teenagers came to the house with Dwight in the lead, it was certain not to be a quiet evening at home."[26]

When not around women, Eisenhower was self-assured but never conceited, and had no use for others who acted vainly. Although he was never a disciplinary problem, Eisenhower recalled that his school deportment was less than model and more than once resulted in reports to the superintendent of schools, a no-nonsense gentleman who regarded discipline as important as academics.[27] According to Lelia Picking, whenever he was called on to recite, he invariably did so. "I never heard him say, 'I don't know.' "[28] Eisenhower earned very respectable grades, particularly during his junior and senior years, when he scored high in every subject but Latin, even though he possessed the potential to have done even better academically.[29]

Another classmate remembered Eisenhower as "a happy sort of fellow . . . every time I'd see him, he'd be laughing [and] kidding with the fellows."[30] He seemed intuitively to sense his strengths. Milton believed that his brother's mind most closely resembled that of their father, "because it was completely logical." One who knew him well at Abilene High School remembers a well-built young man ("strong as an ox") who was never afraid of work and did so without complaint. His mind was quick and inquiring as long as the subject interested him. Otherwise he became bored and disinterested.

A sure sign of Eisenhower's short attention span for a subject he disliked or that bored him was repeated scribblings of his name in his Latin book. He had little patience with teachers he deemed incompetent, and would express his disdain by asking pointed questions designed mostly to embarrass or humiliate. Although utterly tactless, these schoolboy displays were the first signs of Eisenhower's most impressive qualities, which set him apart from his classmates and which would prove to be priceless assets in his future career as an army officer: the ability to remember everything he read or that was shown to him, to listen well, and invariably to ask the right questions.[31]

One of Eisenhower's lifelong habits was to write private evaluations of his superiors and, during World War II, of his principal subordinate officers. The practice had its origins in Abilene High School. Several of his schoolbooks survive and are marked by his scrawls in the margins. In his German book, for example, he graded his teachers as either "good" or "cross." One was scorned as "nothing." Another "cross" teacher was Alice Gentry, who taught algebra and recalled Eisenhower as "an earnest, studious boy, interested in baseball."[32] Miss Gentry's standing with her pupil was undoubtedly exacerbated by the fact that although he enjoyed mathematics, Eisenhower thoroughly despised algebra, and his disinterest was reflected in erratic test scores, which ranged from a failing to a very respectable 95.[33]

Plane geometry was one of the subjects taught during his junior and senior years. Eisenhower found himself attracted to its logic and consistently scored nearly perfect marks in what he has described as "an intellectual adventure." He was so good that the principal made an unusual deal with Eisenhower: They would take away his textbook and let him solve the problems on his own. He accepted the challenge with alacrity and in return was promised an A+ grade if the teacher elected to terminate the experiment.[34]

However, it was the study of ancient history that dominated Eisenhower's interest from an early age. An entire chapter of his memoir is devoted to recounting his enduring love affair with history. His friend John Long recalled that from an early age Eisenhower displayed an unusual interest in history. When Japan invaded Russia in 1904, "Dwight and I used to follow the latest reports and comments on the war in the *Literary Digest*, which Dwight brought to school. . . . [He] was very much interested in every move or detail of the Russian-Japanese War."[35]

Eisenhower idolized George Washington for his courage and daring, and for his brilliant speeches. He avidly studied accounts of Princeton, Trenton, and Valley Forge, and was amazed by what he deemed the stupidity of Washington's enemies, who campaigned for his removal as commander in chief of the Revolutionary Army. Eisenhower combined his extraordinary memory with his father's fascination with Greece, and became so conversant with Greek and Roman history that, until old age, he would instantly interrupt and correct anyone who failed to identify correctly a historical date or missed an element of an important battle or campaign.

Among the ancients, Eisenhower's principal hero was Hannibal, not only for his military daring but for his mastery of the logistics of his times. He marveled how Hannibal had managed to survive as a historical icon despite being portrayed badly by a legion of unfriendly historians and biographers. His other "white hats" included Caesar, Socrates, Pericles, and Themistocles. The "black hats" included Darius, Brutus, Xerxes, and the evil Roman emperor Nero.

In 1967 Eisenhower was visited at his Gettysburg farm by former army chief of staff Gen. Harold K. Johnson. During their conversation Johnson said, "Herodotus wrote about the Peloponnesian War that one cannot be an armchair general twenty miles from the front." Afterward one of his former White House speechwriters, who had been present, asked Eisenhower if he knew the precise wording of the quote. He replied, "First, it wasn't Herodotus but Aemilius Paulanus. Second, it was not the Peloponnesian War, but the Punic War with Carthage. And third, he misquoted." Asked why he hadn't corrected General Johnson, Eisenhower replied, "I got where I did by knowing how to hide my ego and hide my intelligence. I knew the actual quote, but why should I embarrass him?"[36]

At first Eisenhower was content merely to absorb the writings of historians. "As a boy, I never played the prophet, . . . I read history for history's sake, for myself alone."[37] Eisenhower read history so voraciously that he began noticeably neglecting his household duties, to the point that Ida felt obliged to lock up his books in a cabinet. She ought to have known that her strong-willed son would not be deterred from his passion. He soon found the key Ida had hidden, and whenever she left the house, he raided the cabinet to retrieve and read a history book.

It would come as no surprise to those who knew him that he would one day retire to a home on the edge of the Gettysburg battlefield. During his youth the Civil War was still too recent to have generated the enormous body of literature it now has. However, as he grew older it became a fountain of interest. Eisenhower especially empathized with the awesome responsibility of the Union commander at Gettysburg, Gen. George Gordon Meade. At the time of his greatest test as a military commander in June 1944, Eisenhower would draw solace from his knowledge of Meade at Gettysburg.[38] Another of Eisenhower's greatest boyhood heroes was Teddy Roosevelt. "To me he seemed to typify integrity, patriotism and moral courage. . . . in my eyes he was a glamorous figure."[39]

During the same period that Eisenhower was developing his affinity for history, a young blond-haired cadet at West Point by the name of George S. Patton, Jr., was similarly engrossed in the study of history and its consequences. Although the two could not have been more disparate in temperament, Patton's own childhood education in Southern California was dominated by a corresponding passion for history that was the centerpiece of his intellectual life. Like Eisenhower, Patton was tutored on the Bible and could recite passages from memory by the hour. The two studied the same commanders of antiquity but drew different conclusions.

In a small black notebook Patton recorded his thoughts, and throughout his colorful military career constantly drew historical parallels to situations he faced. His frequent exhortation to his soldiers was, "To be a successful soldier you must know history," while Eisenhower regarded the study and practice of history as not only an essential means of learning about war but as the study of the triumph of good over evil. Patton rated the commanders of history by what they accomplished with the forces at their disposal. The "black hats" were those who, in Patton's judgment, failed to measure up or who displayed weakness. Eisenhower never had a great deal to say about Alexander the Great, while Patton scorned him because "in a fit of drunkenness [he] took his own life and his empire fell to pieces."[40]

School was meant to be a place of learning, and there was little interest on the part of the school authorities in promoting or supporting athletics. Football was not sanctioned until Eisenhower's senior year. The initiative was left to the students, and there was sometimes a problem finding enough players to make up a team. The baseball team had real uniforms with AHS inscribed on their shirts, but each football player had to supply his own homemade equipment, usually a sweater and duck pants with some padding added. Football was played without helmets and was not a sport for the faint of heart.[41]

During his high school years Eisenhower blossomed as an athlete. His unusually large hands helped his athleticism immensely. In the autumn of 1908 Eisenhower was elected president of the newly revived Athletic Association, which was organized by the students to raise funds to support the baseball and football teams. For the first time he had been selected to carry out a formal responsibility. Eisenhower worked diligently but learned early on that petty politics within the membership undermined its effectiveness. The experience taught him how difficult it could be to meet the challenge of leading a diverse group of individuals, each of whom had his or her own ideas how things ought to be done. His proudest achievement was writing a constitution that he hoped would insure the association's survival.[42]

Eisenhower played baseball and football during his last two years at Abilene High. No matter the sport, he played with abandon and utter disregard for his own safety. During baseball season he usually played center field, and Edgar, the team captain, was the first baseman.[43] During their senior year Edgar was the fullback, and Dwight played right end in an abbreviated, four-game football season. As president of the Athletic Association, Eisenhower wrote the "Athletics" entry in the school yearbook. His great love of sports shined through when he wrote, "After the football season closed, we had to spend the winter dreaming of past victories and future glories."[44]

Since he was one of the school's most influential athletes, his word carried considerable weight. On one occasion, when the football team traveled to another town for a game, his teammates objected to playing because of the presence of a black athlete on the opposing team. In his typically unequivocal manner, Eisenhower lectured his teammates that this was no excuse for failing to play the game and threatened to go home and play no more that season. They listened, and the game was played. Both before and after the game Eisenhower made a point of shaking the black player's hand.[45] Although he was too young to understand fully what he had done, Eisenhower had just demonstrated a flair for leadership.

Graduation week ceremonies at Abilene High School included the senior class play. Both Edgar and Dwight took part in an outlandish spoof of Shakespeare's *The Merchant of Venice*. Edgar was cast as the Duke of Venice, and Dwight appeared in face paint and a comical costume as a bumbling servant, Launcelot Gobbo. For the only time in their high school careers, Dwight overshadowed his brother. A newspaper review called him "the best amateur humorous character seen on the Abilene stage in this generation and gave an impression that many professionals fail to reach."[46] It was the first and only theater production in which Eisenhower ever participated.

Throughout his high school years he appeared in the yearbook as David Dwight Eisenhower. Only when he entered West Point were the two names unofficially transposed. For the remainder of his life he was Dwight David Eisenhower.

When he graduated on May 27, 1909, he was a far different young man from the gangly youth of 1904.[47] Eighteen-year-old Dwight Eisenhower had grown into a rugged, handsome young man standing five feet eleven inches, his 145-pound body toughened by years of sports and strenuous physical labor.

Eisenhower's entry in the school yearbook, the *Helianthus* (Latin for "sunflower"), described him as the "best historian and mathematician." Edgar was written up as "the greatest football player of the class." It was customary to publish class prophecies for each graduate. The author, Agnes Curry, ventured the prediction that Edgar would become a future two-term president of the United States, while she thought Dwight would become a professor of history at Yale.[48]

Although he still had no career goal in life, both Dwight and Edgar were powerfully motivated to attend college. They were encouraged by the words of the commencement speaker, Henry J. Allen, the editor of the *Wichita Beacon* (later a governor of Kansas and a U.S. senator), who extolled the importance of self-reliance and a college education. "I would sooner begin life over again with one arm cut off than attempt to struggle without a college education," he told them. With Edgar and Dwight, Henry Allen was preaching to the converted.

By 1909 Dwight Eisenhower had outgrown his Abilene roots. His future had yet to be determined, but it clearly lay elsewhere. Although Abilene has become virtually synonymous with the Eisenhower name, behind the later praise and public affection for his hometown lay unforgettable memories of hard times. In his old age Eisenhower reflected a certain weariness at the burdens he had carried, once ruminating how he wished he could return to Abilene and "just be a boy again. How nice that would be."[49] Time changes and often dims memories, but in 1909 Eisenhower's ambition was simply to escape the same fate that had befallen their father.

Even though Dwight's overall grades in high school were well above average, no one seems to have sensed that he would ever become anyone special. Yet high school had kindled a powerful belief that education was the handmaiden to future professional success. The more immediate problem of what direction his life would take was now acute. Unless some means of furthering their educations could be found, both Dwight and Edgar appeared doomed to follow in David's footsteps at the Belle Springs Creamery. There was no money to educate even one brother, much less six. During the summer of 1909, "Ed and I had just one idea . . . to get our hands on every cent we could possibly earn."[50] Their futures looked bleak.

Part II

THE ACCIDENTAL SOLDIER, 1910–1916

5.

Abilene to West Point

I think his grin saved Ike a lot of trouble.

—JOSEPH W. HOWE
editor, Dickinson County News

The same year Dwight Eisenhower graduated from Abilene High School, George S. Patton graduated from West Point with a commission in the cavalry and a clear conviction that he would one day become a famous general. Eisenhower had no idea what he would do with his life. What Eisenhower lacked in 1909 was not determination but merely a vision of what occupation he would pursue or how he would go about it. He received encouragement to continue his education from Charlie Harger, who offered him a job on his newspaper. Eisenhower declined, saying: "No, that is a place for Milton; he is a student." Milton possessed an inquiring mind and a formidable intellect but was frail and had none of the physical toughness of his older brothers. "The older boys enjoyed teasing Milton and making him cry, while at the same time they were determined to make him into a tough-guy imitation of themselves." To help toughen him up, Edgar once locked him in a dark attic, inducing instead a dread of darkness that haunted Milton for many years.[1] Because of their eight-year age difference, Dwight and Milton were never particularly close as children. But as adults the two forged a bond that never existed in their relationships with the other four Eisenhower brothers. "Milton has the brains of the Eisenhower family," Dwight once declared.[2]

David and Ida never foisted their ideas or beliefs onto their six sons. They were taught not only to think for themselves but to choose their own paths in life. Their fierce competitiveness notwithstanding, Edgar and Dwight were in full accord in their resolve to attain a higher education as a means of escaping the drudgery of life in Abilene.[3] Each was resolutely determined to help the other somehow achieve a prized college education. The problem was how to pay for it. The two made a pact: As the eldest, Edgar would be afforded the opportunity to pursue his dream while Dwight worked for a year to raise funds to assist him. Then it would be Dwight's turn for a year. The two would alternate work and school until each graduated eight years later. Edgar was committed to becoming a lawyer and set his sights on the University of Michigan, which he believed had the best law school in the country. Initially Dwight intended to follow Edgar to Michigan, although he had no specific goal in mind other than a college education and a chance to continue playing football and baseball.

The only time David ever spoke openly about one of his children's future careers was his attempt to sway Edgar by offering financial help on the condition he study medicine at the University of Kansas. Edgar rebuffed his father's offer just as David had adamantly spurned Jacob's advice twenty-five years earlier. "There I was, on my own, without a dime," recalled Edgar. With no place else to turn, he approached his uncle, Chris Musser, who offered his patronage as a director of the Farmers National Bank, by personally guaranteeing repayment of a two-hundred-dollar loan that sent Edgar on his way to the University of Michigan. Neither bothered to inform David of the arrangement.[4]

Eisenhower later vehemently disavowed biographer Kenneth Davis's assertion that he spent the years 1910–11 in "aimless drifting."[5] Shortly before his death, Eisenhower chided some of his biographers who had suggested he didn't know what he wanted to do with his life, as "the craziest thing I ever heard of. I was going to go to school but I had to get some money. And I stayed out of school two years in order to help my brother [Edgar]."[6]

Eisenhower's after-school and summer jobs included picking apples, working in a lumberyard and coal yard, and as a straw boss in a small plant that manufactured steel grain bins. He also worked harvesting wheat from dawn to dusk for fifty cents a day. After two years Eisenhower was told he was too big for the job and too small for another. He later described the experience as "my first lesson that relations are governed by neither fixed rules nor logic. . . . For years I had been taught that it takes two to start a quarrel. Now, I saw that in any organized effort there may be as many disagreements about policy and practice as there are participants."[7]

By 1910 Eisenhower had given up his various other jobs for a better-paying full-time position at the Belle Springs Creamery, where his principal duty was to operate the ice tank, from which he had to extract three-hundred-pound blocks of ice with steel tongs and send them down a chute into the ice storage room, then help load them into wagons or boxcars. In summer he could usually be found barefoot, with his sleeves rolled up. On a slow night friends might drop by to play penny-ante poker or help raid the company food locker for ice cream or eggs. They also cooked chickens "on a well-scrubbed shovel in the boiler room."[8]

He was soon promoted to fireman. His responsibilities were to stoke the coal-fired boilers and remove and extinguish hot embers; it was hot, dirty, and unrewarding work. Edgar had once held the same job for less pay and never forgot the "terrible heat," exacerbated by outside temperatures of over one hundred degrees in summer, the sweating, the filth, and the physically exhausting exertion required to load an average of three tons of coal per day. "In this small inferno, life lost its charm but the job led to another promotion," remembered Dwight. During his last year there, in 1910–11, Eisenhower was again advanced, this time to second engineer, and during his last three months earned sixty dollars per month, a salary he deemed impressive. Indeed, Eisenhower's salary was nearly double what his father earned when he was first employed at the creamery in 1892.[9] In return, he worked eighty-four hours per week, from six P.M. to six A.M. in the ice plant.[10] True to his word, Dwight sent Edgar two hundred dollars in 1910. (Years later Edgar mentioned to a friend that he still owed his brother for his share of helping finance his education. Asked why he had not repaid the debt, Edgar replied, "Dwight hasn't asked for it.")[11]

In addition to his work at the creamery, Eisenhower played semipro baseball under an assumed name in another nearby town before entering West Point. For reasons he never explained, it was not until 1961 that Eisenhower finally admitted that he had in fact played professional baseball for one season under a pseudonym (possibly Wilson). He refused to go into detail because it was "too complicated," and ordered his staff not to answer questions on the subject.[12]

Eisenhower's future course was aided immensely by his friendship with a younger classmate named John F. "Six" McDonnell, a talented athlete who played for the high school team and eventually became a successful semipro pitcher. Eisenhower got in the habit of visiting the offices of the weekly newspaper, the *Dickinson County News*, where McDonnell worked part-time for editor Joseph W. Howe.

Howe was a member of the school board, a state senator, and a man of some influence who headed the Dickinson County Democratic Party Committee. The windows of Howe's office were plastered with newspapers from places such as New York, Kansas City, and St. Louis. Eisenhower would avidly devour each while waiting for Six McDonnell to get off work. Howe had set aside a room in the back of the newspaper as a recreational place where young men could meet, read, or just shoot the breeze. Sometimes Eisenhower and his friends boxed to let off steam. Howe remembered him as a good boxer. "He was not revengeful. He never went out looking for trouble, but . . . he never ran away from it. I think his grin saved Ike a lot of trouble." Howe greatly admired that Eisenhower displayed a distinct lack of bitterness about his poverty or his hard work at any job he could find.[13]

The greatest benefit from Eisenhower's friendship with Howe was that he was given access to the books in Howe's sizable library. Abilene had no public library, and Howe's books became a prime source for high school research papers and for learning about the world outside Abilene. One of them was

The Life of Hannibal, a book that ignited Eisenhower's great interest in Hannibal's exploits.

Another of the places frequented by McDonnell and Eisenhower was a nearby pool hall. Even in the early days of the century, pool halls had an unsavory reputation. Yet, for young men like Dwight Eisenhower and Six McDonnell, they were a haven in a small, conservative town like Abilene. "The pool hall was my country club and it also was Dwight's," said McDonnell.[14]

Joe Howe was impressed by this intelligent young man who was better educated and poised than he himself knew. Howe became both a friend and mentor and was undoubtedly responsible for encouraging Eisenhower to pursue the possibility of obtaining a free education at West Point or Annapolis. From his association with Howe, Eisenhower learned about the vast world outside Abilene. For a young man who had never been out of Kansas, it came as a revelation that can only have enhanced Eisenhower's desire to seek his destiny elsewhere. The two frequently engaged in political discussions and debates. Eisenhower had the knack of knowing when to speak and when to keep quiet. Recalled Howe, "He liked to debate subjects and had the faculty of asking controversial questions . . . to confuse his opponent. . . . [If] cornered he would come forth with some witticism and put on his best smile. In that way he generally ended the debate by disposing of his opponent's argument."[15]

Although Eisenhower was too young to have any genuine political persuasion, Howe was convinced that his young friend was a Democrat.[16] Undoubtedly at Howe's instigation, Eisenhower was one of three young men invited to speak at the annual banquet of the Dickinson County Young Men's Democratic Club on November 9, 1909. Whether or not he took the speech seriously is not known, but an indication may be the fact that Eisenhower did not write it until the night before in Howe's back room. He titled it "The Student in Politics," and in it Eisenhower "drew the Republican party as the party of privilege, the Democratic party as the party of the people, and concluded that the only course for a young man who was a student of politics was to vote for the Democrats." It was a remarkable performance for a young man with no previous training in public speaking or speech writing.[17]

Howe would later express the conviction that Eisenhower had given a decidedly Democratic speech. "I'm certain," he said, "that the young Dwight I knew in Abilene thought of himself as a Democrat," like his father, David, who was a registered member of the party.[18] When Eisenhower ran for president as a Republican in 1952, Howe wrote bitterly to Six McDonnell that he felt betrayed by Eisenhower's decision.[19] Perhaps his displeasure reached Eisenhower's ears, but in his memoir, *At Ease*, he fails to acknowledge or even mention Joe Howe's important contributions at a key juncture in his life.

Dwight Eisenhower's own recollections suggest that he first began to consider attending the U.S. Naval Academy at Annapolis in 1910 at the urging of his friend Everett E. "Swede" Hazlett, Jr. Eisenhower had first met Hazlett, a physician's son, in 1905, when he was a sophomore and Hazlett a freshman at Abilene High School. Perhaps recollecting his own childhood nickname, he dubbed the blond youth "Swede," a name that stuck for the rest of his life. Hazlett was a well-built young man who had no interest in either sports or fighting. As a north-side boy from a prosperous family, Swede had led a more sheltered life. Despite his size Swede became the target of school bullies until Eisenhower intervened to put an end to such shenanigans. The two became close friends, but after a year their budding friendship was put on hold when Hazlett left Abilene to attend a military academy in Wisconsin. Eisenhower did not see him again until the summer of 1910.[20]

From the time he was twelve, Hazlett loved to ride horses and actually coveted an appointment to West Point and a career in the cavalry, whose home base was at nearby Fort Riley. Dr. Hazlett had sent Swede to Wisconsin in an effort to "cure" him of his desire to pursue a career that was then held in low esteem. The plan backfired after Hazlett became even more enthusiastic, although ultimately unable to obtain an appointment to West Point. Instead, thanks to his family's influence, he was tendered an appointment to Annapolis in the spring of 1910 by the local congressman, Rep. Roland R. Rees. When he returned to Abilene in June, Eisenhower learned that his friend had failed the mathematics portion of the Annapolis entrance examination, and was home to retake the test and pursue a reappointment.

During the summer of 1910 Hazlett regaled his friend with tales of life outside Kansas, and suggested that Eisenhower should pursue an appointment to Annapolis. Eisenhower was easily convinced. "He got to telling me about these two academies (West Point and Annapolis) and he got me steamed up about it." Moreover, Hazlett reminded him, if Eisenhower managed to secure an appointment to Annapolis, it would mean they would become classmates, making their ordeal of surviving for four years more tolerable.

Eisenhower wrote to Representative Rees, who replied that he had no further vacancies but suggested he contact Sen. Joseph L. Bristow, who had been elected to the U.S. Senate in 1908 and was the only Kansas legislator who had one vacancy to each school to fill in 1911.[21] Eisenhower immediately wrote to Bristow on August 20, 1910:

> Dear Sir:
> I would very much like to enter either the school at Annapolis, or the one at West Point. In order to do this, I must have an appointment to one of these places and so I am writing to you in order to secure the same.

> I have graduated from high school and will be nineteen years of age this fall [*sic*].
>
> If you find it possible to appoint me to one of these schools, your kindness will certainly be appreciated by me.
>
> Trusting to hear from you, concerning this matter, at your earliest convenience, I am, respectfully yours,
>
> Dwight Eisenhower.[22]

Although Bristow never replied to his letter, Eisenhower set out to obtain sponsorship for his nomination.[23] As well as securing the support of Democrat Joe Howe, he solicited and received letters of recommendation from both factions of the Abilene Republican party: Charlie Harger, editor of the *Abilene Daily Reflector,* and Phil Heath, editor of the more liberal Republican *Abilene Chronicle*, a remarkable feat for a rather unsophisticated young man. Eisenhower also visited virtually every Abilene business and civic leader, and his efforts paid off with a number of other letters supporting his nomination.

A mere two weeks after his first letter to Bristow, Eisenhower again wrote rather forcefully to ask for the senator's consideration. "Some time ago [*sic*], I wrote to you applying for an appointment to West Point or Annapolis. As yet I have heard nothing definite from you about the matter, but I noticed in the daily papers that you would soon give a competitive examination for these appointments. Now, if you find it impossible to give me an appointment outright, to one of these places, would I have the right to enter this competitive examination?"[24]

Yes, indeed, replied Bristow. The examination was to be held on October 4 and 5 in Topeka, which left Eisenhower a mere three weeks to prepare. Fortunately the night shift at Belle Springs Creamery provided time for Eisenhower to study for the examination. With Swede's help "the two of us began studying together, and we did it by getting the old examinations that these schools had been putting out for years. They had the answers, so we studied and reexamined each other." A decade later at Camp Meade, Maryland, Eisenhower would employ the same technique to study battlefield problems used in the army's Command and General Staff School at Fort Leavenworth with his charismatic new friend, Col. George S. Patton, Jr. He had never before studied as diligently as he did during September 1910. Night after night the two crammed for the examination and tested each other. Years later Swede would remember that Eisenhower's "God-given brain had sped him along" to the point where the pupil had forged ahead of his teacher.[25]

Eisenhower's hard work soon paid off. Eight candidates participated in the two-day examination. He was one of four who kept his options open by indicating he would accept either West Point or Annapolis, while the other four applied only for West Point. When the results were tallied, Eisenhower had finished second overall by only a slim margin with a score of 87.5. The top candidate, George Pulsifer, Jr., scored 89.5 but because Pulsifer had specified only West Point, it meant that Eisenhower had finished as the top candidate for Annapolis.

Senator Bristow decided not to tender Eisenhower an appointment to Annapolis. Instead he wrote on October 24 to announce that Eisenhower was his nominee for the vacancy at West Point in 1911, and his name would be forwarded to the secretary of war. The letter required that Eisenhower furnish "a statement of your exact age, years and months, and a statement as to how long you have been an actual resident of Kansas." In his reply the following day thanking the senator for the appointment, Eisenhower either lied or again misstated his age: "I am just nineteen years [*sic*] and eleven days of age and have been a resident of Kansas for eighteen years," he wrote.[26]

What Eisenhower never knew was that Bristow had sent his friend Phil Heath the applications of all the candidates and asked for his recommendations. Heath had placed Eisenhower's name first for the West Point vacancy, which explains why Bristow passed over Pulsifer in favor of Eisenhower. It turned out to be a stroke of good fortune for Eisenhower. The rules for admission to Annapolis required that a candidate must enter before his twentieth birthday. Thus, had Bristow appointed him to Annapolis, Eisenhower could not legally have accepted, even though he had finished first.

Bristow's decision now meant that Eisenhower had only to pass the West Point entrance and physical exams, without which the appointment would default to Pulsifer. His parents were not overjoyed by the news but kept their silence. Eisenhower attempted to sugarcoat it by observing he had yet to pass an examination others had had far more time to prepare for. He borrowed one of Howe's books, called *Century Book of Facts*, to study for the forthcoming West Point exam, remarking that "he guessed he would have to do some real studying now."[27] Minnie Stewart thought Eisenhower was wasting his talents. "There's just no *future* in the Army," she said. "You're just throwing yourself away." This time it was Eisenhower who kept silent.[28]

To better prepare himself Eisenhower returned to Abilene High School in the autumn of 1910 to take refresher classes in math and physics. With no eligibility rules in those days, it was also a grand opportunity to play another year of football, this time as a tackle. During a game with archrival Salina, Eisenhower is alleged to have ferociously leveled an opponent in retaliation after the Abilene quarterback, Six McDonnell, was accidentally knocked unconscious. It was actually a teammate who had reciprocated, but the tale became another of the fanciful legends about Eisenhower.[29]

The West Point entrance examination was held in January 1911. Eisenhower traveled to Jefferson Barracks, Missouri, an army post on the outskirts of St. Louis, where the test was administered over four days. It marked the farthest he had ever been from Abilene. Both Eisenhower and Pulsifer passed the written and physical examinations. Eisenhower was ordered to report to West Point in June 1911 as a member of the class of 1915.[30]

(In July 1911 a young man from rural Missouri who was likewise too poor to afford a higher education reported to Jefferson Barracks to take the grueling entrance examination as an alternate candidate from his congressional district. He left St. Louis believing he had failed miserably. Three weeks later he was astonished to learn he had not only passed but that the principal candidate had failed some parts of the exam and had been disqualified. As the alternate, he was to report immediately to join the class of 1915 at West Point. His name was Omar Nelson Bradley.)

Eisenhower later gave full credit to Swede Hazlett for alerting him to the opportunities offered by West Point and Annapolis. "As you well know, it was only through you that I ever heard of the Government academies." The truth is that well before the summer of 1910 Eisenhower already knew all about West Point and Annapolis, both through conversations with Joe Howe and, much earlier, with his close boyhood friend, John E. Long. According to Long, "I spent more time with him than I spent with any other boy." The two often spoke of how they might obtain a free education. "We often planned and talked about going to Annapolis to get an [college] education. . . . as we were both too poor." After moving to Lawrence, Long later took the Annapolis entrance exam and failed it badly. He wrote to Eisenhower advising, "Please don't take that examination until you're well prepared."[31]

Ida Eisenhower was dismayed by the news her son would attend West Point. "She didn't like it," said her most mercurial son, "but she never made the fuss about it that some people have tried to [suggest]—she just thought that for one of her boys to go into the Army [and] have something to do with war . . . [was] rather wicked. And I know that she was sad."[32] Dwight's decision went to the heart of her deeply held beliefs, which had less to do with pacifism than they did with Witness theology, which holds that all war is wrong. However, Ida's true reservation was the fact that she was obliged to hide from her six sons "her 'weakened faith' and 'grief' that resulted from Dwight Eisenhower's pursuit of a military career."[33]

The day he left home to board a train at the nearby Abilene terminal to begin the long journey to West Point, Eisenhower remembered bidding a hasty good-bye to his mother "before I started bawling." Milton was the only son present and vividly remembers, "Mother stood there like a stone statue, and I stood right by her until Ike was out of sight. Then she came in and went to her room and bawled like a baby. . . . I cried too."[34]

6.

The Long Gray Line

From the first day at West Point, and any number of times thereafter, I often asked myself: What am I doing here?

Eisenhower's journey by rail to West Point evoked mixed emotions. Although driven to leave Abilene and continue his education, there was the unease and fear that comes with being abruptly wrenched from the security of a close-knit family. Other than his brief trip to St. Louis to take the West Point entrance exam earlier in 1911, Eisenhower had never seen a big city.

During a stopover in Chicago he was reunited with Ruby Norman, who was a student at the Chicago Conservatory of Music. They spent several carefree days exploring the sights of the city and attending films at night. Ruby was the only person outside members of his family whom Eisenhower had ever confided in, and during the next four years she would become not only a pen pal but a sounding board for his triumphs and tribulations.

Eisenhower then detoured to Ann Arbor for a brief reunion with Edgar at the University of Michigan. One evening the two rented a canoe and, with two coeds in tow, paddled leisurely on a nearby river to the accompaniment of popular tunes of the day played on Edgar's portable phonograph. Eisenhower called it the most romantic evening he had ever known, although it left him envious of his brother's status and apprehensive that he might have erred in not following in Edgar's footsteps.[1] The two brothers would not see each other again until 1926.

Eisenhower's inexperience of big cities left him "scared to death" at the thought of stopping in New York. His trepidations were somewhat assuaged by the presence on the train of a number of other new cadets, many of whom displayed their collective uncertainty. The train stopped at the village of Highland Falls, forty-five miles north of New York City on the morning of June 14, 1911. On a typically hot and steamy summer day, Dwight Eisenhower, like so many others before him, made the trek with a heavy suitcase up the steep hill from the railway station to the place where "I really hit a new world." Within the space of several hours his life would be turned upside down.

First established in 1775 as a military fortress, West Point still retained many characteristics from its grim origins dating to the Revolutionary War. Situated astride a sharp bend in the Hudson River, the fort had been a strategically important outpost of the fledgling nation, and the ideal site from which to prevent the British fleet from occupying the Hudson River Valley and possibly suppressing the budding Revolution. West Point's elaborate defenses included guns mounted on the parapets overlooking the river, which at one time had a great chain across it. George Washington once called West Point "the key to the continent."[2] In 1780 its commander was Benedict Arnold—the hero of the historic battles of Fort Ticonderoga, Quebec, and Saratoga—once rated "the most brilliant soldier of the Continental Army," who became the archbetrayer of the American Revolution.

In the century before Eisenhower arrived there as a cadet, West Point had evolved from a school for engineers that had graduated a mere two officers in 1802 to a national institution that supplied the U.S. Army with the majority of its professional officers. The top graduates became engineer and artillery officers, while the middle and bottom ranks of each class found themselves commissioned in the infantry. Thus, when Robert E. Lee finished second in the class of 1829 he became an engineer, while Grant, who finished in the middle of his class, was relegated to the infantry.[3]

During the Civil War the armies of the Union and the Confederacy were dominated by its graduates, which in addition to Grant and Lee included George McClellan, Abner Doubleday, George G. Meade, J. E. B. Stuart, Philip H. Sheridan, William Tecumseh Sherman, Stonewall Jackson, Joe Johnston, Ambrose Burnside, Jefferson Davis, and the "goat" (lowest ranking) of the class of 1861, an intensely ambitious young officer named George Armstrong Custer. Although the Civil War pitted West Point classmates against one another, it failed either to seriously disrupt the academy's mission or to prevent those who fought for the Confederacy from eventually sending their sons there in the post–Civil War years.

During this period the practice of hazing became an integral part of plebe life, and a West Point tradition. Its excesses included strenuous and often harmful physical exercise, liberal doses of Tabasco sauce in a plebe's food, and being forced to participate in elaborate funeral ceremonies for dead rats. Hazing produced a code of silence on the part of the hapless plebes, and it became a matter of dishonor to expose the upperclassmen who perpetrated such mischief. Among those who was hazed unmercifully as a cadet was a 1903 graduate named Douglas MacArthur, an officer who would one day play a pivotal role in the military career of Dwight Eisenhower.[4]

At the start of the twentieth century the U.S. Military Academy was considerably smaller than the present imposing facility. In 1911 Eisenhower and the other incoming members of the class of 1915 entered a world little changed from that of the remote nineteenth-century outpost. There to greet them rudely with shouts, abuse, and instructions were upper-class cadre, some of whom were yearlings (sophomores) newly liberated from their own year of hell as plebes. The arrival of a new class marked the start of what is still inelegantly dubbed "beast barracks," a rite of passage designed to indoctrinate civilians in the West Point way and to identify and weed out those unable or unwilling to function as future officers. The cadet yearbook still referred to plebes as "scum of the earth."

West Point has been aptly described as "a military monastery" whose occupants "were isolated from the outside diseases of commercialism and money-grubbing."[5] MacArthur once likened it to "a provincial reformatory based on fear,"[6] and in fact four years at West Point were their own form of penal servitude, eased only by a two-month leave the summer after the second class year, and a Christmas leave or two for those in high academic standing.

The entire corps of cadets consisted of 650 young men organized as "the Battalion," which consisted of six companies, A through F, commanded by a quartermaster. Of the 287 cadets who constituted the class of 1915 (at the time West Point's largest plebe class), only 162 actually graduated—an attrition rate of 44 percent. Moreover, Eisenhower's class was hardly a representative cross section of young American men. Most were predominantly Protestants of Anglo-Saxon Irish, English, Scottish, or German origin.

Discipline verged on the Draconian and was ruthlessly enforced in the form of demerits for infractions of the rules and regulations. Excessive demerits earned the offender punishment tours marched with military precision twice weekly for two hours, with rifle and pack. Serious offenses required a personal explanation to the commandant of cadets, about 90 percent of which were rejected. "It hardly seems possible," remembered Col. Joseph C. Haw, a graduate of the class of 1915, "that a grown man was actually reported for touching a lady's arm, but it is an undisputable fact. So zealously did the Tactical Department guard our manners and morals that a contemporary of ours was actually 'skinned' [assessed demerits] for assisting his own mother across the street."[7] Other offenses included "strong odor of perfume in room," "displaying indifference at [horseback] riding," and "highly unmilitary conduct . . . allowing a guard tent to be used for the amusement of ladies." Despite its rigidity and provincialism, "we managed to have lots of fun . . . out of the little daily incidents of cadet life," recalled Haw. " 'Kidding' and 'razzing' were almost too incessant and intense, for there was little else to joke about."[8]

The West Point method of turning a civilian into a professional soldier was autocratic. Hazing still occurred but had been made punishable by dismissal, and the treatment of plebes was generally restricted to the more traditional, less harmful harassments. Young men were stripped of their civilian mores and over four years the makings of an officer and a gentleman were created. Yet despite its minor reforms, West Point remained deeply tradition-bound and set in its ways. The cold and forbidding gray granite buildings of West Point were unlike anything most new arrivals had ever seen. The rooms and living conditions were equally bleak, and the amenities few. The winters were frigid, and the summers hellishly hot.

Eisenhower's enduring recollection of his first day at West Point was of "bewilderment and calculated chaos." Cadets were not permitted to have money and were required to turn in whatever funds they possessed to the bursar to pay a monthly charge levied by the government for uniforms. The new plebes were measured for their uniforms, filled out forms, and hustled from place to place to carry out a timeworn practice. Eisenhower described their rude introduction to cadet life as "a series of shouts and barks" by "self-important upperclassmen."

Plebes were assigned to cadet companies based on height. Eisenhower was assigned to F Company, where the tallest cadets were placed. Late that afternoon, the members of the new class of 1915 assembled in full-dress uniform on the fabled Plain of West Point to participate in the traditional first review of the "long gray line." To the accompaniment of guns firing salutes and the band playing martial music, young men who had been civilians only hours earlier marched awkwardly but proudly and then swore the required oath that officially made them the newest members of the corps of cadets. The sight of the American flag and the pomp of his first military parade deeply moved Eisenhower. For the first time in his life it dawned on him what commitment really meant. "Across a half century," he later wrote, it was "a supreme moment . . . I can look back and see a rawboned, gawky Kansas boy from the farm country earnestly repeating the words that would make him a cadet."[9]

For the next three weeks the newcomers were subjected to the rigors of beast barracks in a tent city established at the edge of the Plain. Until September they were taught the rudiments of military drill and ceremonies and participated in an endless routine of drill, guard duty, inspections, and petty intimidations. Nearly a half century later Eisenhower recalled that in the summer of 1911, "no form of animal life [was] more obnoxious and pestiferous than the ubiquitous cadet instructor."[10] Even so, the heat, the shouting, the necessity for instant obedience to the most banal commands, and the constant drills and harassment by the upperclassmen did not unduly trouble Cadet Eisenhower. His boyhood in Abilene had prepared him well for the physical ordeal of West Point. During his few moments of free time he would often reflect on the comic aspects of life as plebe. He reckoned that if he and his classmates had been given time for contemplation, most would have left West Point aboard the next train to pass through Highland Falls. Not for the first time Eisenhower asked himself, "What am I doing here? Like the other young men, I sometimes wondered—where did I come from, by what route and why; by what chance arrangement of fate did I come by this uniform?"[11] Yet, it was a constant source of comfort that no matter how difficult the ordeal, Eisenhower's education was being paid for by the government. His only major obstacle those first weeks was his difficulty in learning to march properly. Until he finally got the hang of it, Eisenhower was consigned to the aptly named Awkward Squad.

The rituals plebes were taught included saluting all officers. The rule was unambiguous: If in doubt, salute. Soon after his arrival Eisenhower's inexperience proved embarrassing. As the academy band came marching down a street, he encountered "the most decorated fellow I had ever seen. I hesitated just a second, then snapped to attention and presented arms but he did not return the salute. I did it again and a third time before realizing he was the drum major."[12]

Plebes were obliged to memorize the name of every classmate and of every upperclassman. Overall, however, the relationship between the upperclassmen and the plebe class was good-natured, remembers Haw. "The 'plebe' system was well calculated to take the conceit out of a man, and a year of it has cured many a swollen head."[13]

The education of West Point's teachers, all of whom were graduates, was generally restricted to what they had learned as cadets, and was "narrow, formalistic, and unimaginative."[14] Teaching was by rote and there was only the approved "school solution" to an academic problem. Independent thinking was not only discouraged but punished. When Douglas MacArthur became superintendent in 1919, he was determined to revise the curriculum and to prepare future officers for what he was certain would be another world war. "How long are we going on preparing for the War of 1812?" he once remarked.[15] Eisenhower soon learned the lesson that "at West Point we were going to do it West Point's way or we were not going to do it at all."

For all its shortcomings West Point, with its creed of "Duty, Honor, Country," instilled in men like MacArthur, Patton, Eisenhower, and Bradley a profound sense of pride, nostalgia, and commitment that endured for the rest of their lives. Other than athletics, the one aspect of cadet life Eisenhower firmly embraced was the West Point honor code. Then, as now, the heart of West Point life is the honor system, under which a cadet will not lie, cheat, steal, or tolerate those who do. Conviction of an honor offense usually meant automatic dismissal. Cadets typically reported themselves, as Eisenhower once did for an infraction as the officer of the guard.

For one of the first times in his life the drawbacks of being the middle child of a large family paid off. The discipline and petty harassments were physically trying but never even remotely overwhelming. Everyone suffered from the effects of the stupefying heat, but it was the rigid discipline that overwhelmed many, including Eisenhower's first roommate, a young man from Kansas who soon quit. "He had come from this little town as the town hero. They'd put him on a train with the band, the mayor made speeches, and when he had this kind of treatment, this just shocked him and he thought everybody was cutting him to pieces. . . . I tried to tell him that, after all, thousands of boys had gone through this same experience ahead of him but he'd put his head down and weep."[16]

Eisenhower's new roommate ("wife" in the West Point vernacular) turned out to be another Kansan, Paul Alfred Hodgson, who hailed from nearby Wichita. The two instantly bonded, roomed together for the full four years, and thereafter remained close friends for life. P.A., as he was known, was a serious student and a distinguished athlete who starred on the great undefeated football team of 1914. Eisenhower's influence on P.A. was addictive. Normally a studious, sincere young man, Hodgson was not cut from the same devil-may-care cloth as Eisenhower; nevertheless one or the other was in recurring disciplinary trouble. During their four years together, both did time in arrest of quarters for more serious violations and walked punishment tours twice a week, thus joining the ranks of the "area birds." It might have been worse—their shenanigans were as daring as they were numerous. P.A.'s letters to his family began to make flattering references to his new "wife," and Eisenhower said, "The four years we spent in the same room more than a quarter of a century ago are still some of my most treasured memories."[17]

Nevertheless Hodgson recalled with amusement that when it came to performing required minor duties, his roommate "could be a sly one. . . . We were supposed to take turns opening the windows at night and closing them first thing in the morning. But Ike dressed so fast that he could linger in bed—and I, a slower dresser, always had to get out of my warm bed onto the cold floor and close the windows. I was always very careful about cleaning my part of the room whereas Ike was very nonchalant. But, somehow I always got the demerits."[18]

West Point's authoritarian system failed unduly to concern Eisenhower, who dismissed his mediocre disciplinary record by recalling how he simply ignored or evaded the many details required of a cadet. "I couldn't be bothered with such things, and so I got lots of demerits." He readily admitted that while he was far from being a careful cadet, "I was far from being a troublemaker but I didn't think of myself as either a scholar . . . or as a military figure whose professional career might be seriously affected by his academic and disciplinary record."[19]

Eisenhower viewed it as a challenge to violate West Point's strict rules without getting caught. He displayed no fear whatsoever that his conduct might result in dire repercussions, and his escapades ranged from hilarious to downright venturesome. Eisenhower seemed to relish every opportunity to outwit an instructor or upperclassman. An example during his plebe year occurred when he and another cadet were cited for a minor infraction and ordered to appear in a cadet corporal's room in "full-dress coats." The two duly presented themselves clad in only their tunics, under which they were both naked. When ordered to explain himself, Eisenhower replied with a straight face, "Nothing was said about trousers, sir." The prank outraged the corporal and drew the mirth of his roommate. The two plebes were directed to return after taps in full uniform. Their punishment consisted of bracing (a rigid position of attention with one's chin pushed firmly into one's chest) against the wall "until we left our bodily outlines on it in perspiration." Afterward Eisenhower and his fellow plebes had a good but quiet laugh at the corporal's expense.[20]

On another occasion a classmate was hit on the back of his head in the mess hall with a piece of beef. Only Eisenhower's face contained a hint of a smile, and the victim retaliated by heaving a potato at him, "but a poor plebe picked that moment to stand up. He got it right in the eye."[21]

For the most part his transgressions reflected indifference and rebelliousness and ran the gamut of sloppiness, uniform violations, lateness, and other infractions. His laid-back attitude once cost him a hefty five demerits for "smiling in ranks at drill after being corrected."[22] His colorful vocabulary earned him five more for "using profanity at supper." Although Eisenhower's use of profanity did not originate at West Point, it was sufficiently refined during his four-year tenure that it became a permanent part of his persona.

The cadets of F Company were bigger, more athletic, tougher, and inclined to look down on the cadets of the other companies as "runts." Whether it was short-sheeting someone's bed or dumping buckets of water on an unsuspecting cadet, no prank was too small or scheme too audacious that it did not involve Eisenhower.[23] It did not take long for Eisenhower to emerge as one of the most popular cadets in his class. His smile, fun-loving demeanor, and impish disdain for authority were attractive qualities. It was now that the nickname his mother so disliked was first used by his classmates. It stuck for the remainder of his life.

Eisenhower's litany of infractions between 1911 and 1915 fills nearly ten pages. In his senior year alone, he accumulated 100 of his 307 total demerits, thus joining a prestigious group of West Point graduates ranging from J. E. B. Stuart and U. S. Grant ("maltreating a horse—arrested"); Custer ("maltreating new cadet—arrested"); and George McClellan, A. P. Hill, and William T. Sherman ("discharging his musket"), whose names appeared in the commandant's disciplinary register. "My success in compiling a staggering catalogue of demerits," said Eisenhower, "was largely due to a lack of motivation in almost everything other than athletics, except for the simple and stark resolve to get a college education."[24]

Once asked if he ever thought he might not make it through his plebe year, Eisenhower replied, "No, no. I watched my studies and I knew I was going all right. . . . I was very strong and fit physically in those days . . . and when I found I could meet my academic demands, I was all right. I was confident."[25] As he had previously in high school, Eisenhower did not excel academically anywhere near his potential at West Point. Admitting that "I paid no attention" as a cadet, Eisenhower knew he could have done far better. More often than not he would wait until the very last minute to compose papers that were actually remarkably polished pieces of writing. "I'd go to sleep when my roommate would be working. In the morning he'd get up and say, 'Do you know anything about this lesson?' I'd say, 'No, what is it? You tell me.' "[26]

Eisenhower's stubbornness, although sometimes carried to extremes, was also indicative of how important he considered keeping one's word. Classmate James Van Fleet, a future four-star general, remembers how he was razzed by classmates for "bookworming his way to the top" of his English class. Eisenhower responded by pledging not to study an English book outside class for the remainder of the term. "I don't know why he did it," said Van Fleet, but "he finally hit the bottom of the class. But he wouldn't crack a book until the class members released him from his pledge."[27]

One year, several of the hell-raising cadets in Eisenhower's circle were abruptly transferred to other cadet companies by the tactical officers in order "to break up this rabble." Chief among them was Eisenhower. Another self-described "roughneck" was Charles C. Herrick, who recalled that, "One of the worst offenses at the Point was to get caught off the reservation. But somehow it never worried Ike and some of the others. They'd sneak out the lavatory windows, and past the sentry post and off they'd go up the Hudson in a rented boat to Newburgh for coffee and sandwiches. Imagine, they'd travel 30 miles—15 there and 15 back—just for chow. If any of those guys had been caught they'd have been thrown right out of the academy."[28]

Alexander M. "Babe" Weyand, who later earned prominence as an army football player, Olympic wrestler, and noted sports historian, was also a plebe in 1911, and vividly remembers his first encounter with Dwight Eisenhower. One day soon after plebe camp, a cadet entered his room and barked: "Who lives in this house?" Thinking it was an upperclassman, Weyand and his roommate immediately leaped to attention and braced only to find it was a grinning classmate. "In those days, Eisenhower affected a tough breezy western manner. 'At ease,' he barked as he swaggered into the room . . . his smile was so warm and friendly that I had to laugh." Eisenhower and Weyand's roommate "frequently teamed in bizarre enterprises for the sole purpose of annoying the upperclassmen. They were usually caught and disciplined but they had fun while it lasted."[29] Wherever there was mischief, Eisenhower was almost certain to be in the middle. A classmate recalled how, whenever there was a snowball fight, "Ike was always in the thick of it." Cadets would often use the roof of the barracks to gain access to the ground floor after taps. "We would hear a splash of water and everyone knew Ike had caught someone sneaking along the roof below his [third floor] window."[30]

. . .

Eisenhower freely admitted that one of his principal motivations in attending West Point was his expectation that he would be selected to the varsity football and baseball teams. "It would be difficult to overemphasize the importance that I attached to participation in sports," he said. Plebes were eligible for the varsity teams, and with his experience in Abilene he fully expected to be selected. "Ike talked such a grand game," said Weyand, "that we thought he would make the big squad but he was in for a keen disappointment. When the squad was announced Paul Hodgson was on it but Ike was not. To use one of his favorite expressions, he was 'fit to be tied,' as he thought he deserved a place."[31] However, he was deemed too small and light. Instead he played football on the Cullum Hall team, a junior varsity squad that had been created several years earlier by a member of the class of 1904 named Joseph W. Stilwell (the "Vinegar Joe" of future World War II fame). Eisenhower acquitted himself well and helped win the most important game of a short season against a nearby military academy.

Eisenhower did earn a place on the varsity baseball team, but the coach disliked his hitting style and he never played in a single game. He was also selected for the intramural medicine ball team, which comprised the eight cadets judged the fastest. Overall, however, Eisenhower's athletic career at West Point during his plebe year was a major disappointment.

Eisenhower entered West Point in 1911 weighing about 150 pounds, but by the autumn of 1912, between indulging his appetite in the mess hall and engaging in strenuous workouts in the gym, he had bulked up to a very solid 174 pounds in an effort to make the football team. He was still thought to be too light to make the first team, but his hustle, intensity, and "love for hard bodily contact" made a good impression on the coach. The trainer, Sgt. Marty Maher, who spent fifty-five years at West Point, described how "Ike was the first cadet on the field for football practice and the very last to leave. I used to curse him because he would practice so late that I would be collecting footballs he had kicked away in the darkness. He never hit the rubbing table because he would always be out there practicing punts instead of getting a rubdown."[32]

Although he started the 1912 season as a substitute, Eisenhower was soon promoted to the varsity football squad and played in five games as a linebacker on defense and a running back (then called a "plunging back") on offense. Against Colgate he was sent into the game late in the fourth quarter and scored a touchdown, earning praise from the *New York Tribune*, which wrote that "the work of Eisenhower brought joy to the ARMY rooters." Suddenly he was regarded as a talented running back.

His solid play earned him a start as a halfback and linebacker against the Carlisle Indian School, coached by Pop Warner. The star of the Carlisle team was the legendary football great and 1912 decathlon and pentathlon Olympic gold medalist, Jim Thorpe. It usually took at least two defenders to tackle Thorpe, one to hit him high, the other low. On one play he was hammered so hard by Eisenhower and his linebacker partner that Carlisle was obliged to take an injury time-out while Thorpe caught his breath. Eisenhower's happiest memory of playing football was that particular play, when Thorpe "proved as human as any of them." Elation soon turned to dismay, however, when Thorpe niftily averted an attempted gang tackle by Eisenhower and his partner. Instead of tackling Thorpe, the two defenders collided with each other and were so banged up they had to be removed from the game, even though Eisenhower protested that he was well enough to continue. Under the rules neither player could return until the start of the next quarter. Army had scored first, but with its two best linebackers out of action, the game became a rout, which Carlisle won 27–6 in one of the most memorable sporting events in West Point history. After Eisenhower became famous, Babe Weyand asked Jim Thorpe if he recalled the game. "Jim nodded his head vigorously and grunted, 'Good linebacker.' "[33]

Eisenhower's football career came to an abrupt end the following week during a game against Tufts University. He was tackled by the ankle and severely twisted his knee struggling to pick up extra yardage as he was falling. "I could feel something rip although it didn't particularly hurt." After several more plays Eisenhower fell to the ground without being touched. "I couldn't get up, so they took me off the field, and I never got back on as a player again." After he gained prominence, numerous men who claimed to have played that day for Tufts, and to have inflicted Eisenhower's injury, apologized to him at least several dozen times, he laughingly recalled. "I wonder how many men Tufts had on the field when I was hurt?"[34]

The doctors examined his swollen knee but prescribed only rest until the swelling disappeared, leaving Eisenhower convinced he had recovered. Then disaster struck. "The doctors didn't warn me I had a permanently weakened knee. So I went riding" during a voluntary "monkey-drill team" performance, which required dismounting and remounting a horse at the gallop, often facing to the rear. The first time Eisenhower tried it, "I just crashed myself all to pieces."

Eisenhower never challenged biographer Kenneth Davis's version that the injury was precipitated by an allegation of malingering by the riding instructor, and Eisenhower's stubborn refusal to invoke the decision of the doctors that he refrain from participating in riding drills. P. A. Hodgson was said to have attempted to no avail to persuade his defiant roommate not to continue, but Eisenhower was determined to prove the slur wrong. P.A. half-carried, half-dragged him to the infirmary, all the while cursing both "the drillmaster, and Dwight for being a fool . . . when they reached the hospital the doctor cursed too. The knee, red and swollen, was a mess."[35]

Eisenhower spent four agonizing days in the infirmary, where the doctors pronounced the injury permanent. "So I had to give that [athletics] up."[36] His leg was immobilized in a cast, his days as an athlete at an inglorious end; "it was just too hard for me to accept for a while." Head coach Capt. Ernest "Pot" Graves was livid when he learned that Eisenhower had reinjured his knee while riding and would be unavailable to play in the Army-Navy game. "Here I come up with the best line plunger and linebacker I've ever seen at West Point and he busts his knee in the riding hall."[37]

Equitation was the most difficult physical requirement a cadet had to successfully pass and was far more dangerous than football. Most of the horses were former army polo ponies with evil tempers, including one that not only threw its riders but then delighted in kicking them in the face. Once there were three cadets in the infirmary with broken jaws from the same pony. Given the rigors of equitation and the so-called monkey drills, it was hardly surprising that Eisenhower's athletic career ended in 1912.

The senior riding instructor was one of West Point's most eccentric characters, a cavalry major, Julian R. Lindsey, nicknamed "the Squire." Horsemanship was made deliberately difficult: Cadets were obliged to ride with only a saddle pad and a surcingle (a makeshift girth to hold the pad in place). Recalled Joseph Haw, "Some of us fell off our horses so frequently that we could almost tell what part of the riding hall we had fallen by the taste of the tanbark." The following year English saddles were used, but without stirrups. "In those days the cavalry idea was to make riding rough and tough. If a horse refused a jump and catapulted his rider headfirst into the hurdle," the instructor would drawl, " 'You, man, are you trying to break that hurdle?' . . . Not until the middle of our last year were we able to hold the reins when taking a jump."[38]

As the cadets went through the prescribed drills, the Squire would shriek, "That's terrible, [Mr. So-and-so]! Oh, my God, how I suffer! What would the people in Virginia say?" His orderly was a black enlisted man named Hazel, "who was always armed with notebook and pencil. In the midst of his agony at our antics 'the Squire' would yell, 'Report him! Hazel, report that man!' and another 'skin' would go down in Hazel's little black book." The cadets achieved a small measure of retribution by staging a lifelike parody of the two in the annual Hundredth Night Play, a stage revue similar to Eisenhower's high school senior class play. Two impersonators would croon:

For I'm a nut, a nutty nut,
A Hazel nut perhaps.
I'm always fixin' little things
From reveille till taps.[39]

For a time Eisenhower studied scientific boxing, which he thought would aid him in one day finally besting Edgar. He again reinjured the same knee after twisting it while boxing. This too landed him back in the infirmary, as did an injury playing handball in 1913. "He is afraid it is worse than ever," wrote P.A. to his family. "It finishes his chances for ever again playing football. . . . He had to be carried to the hospital. . . . He was certainly a blue boy."[40]

Eisenhower's knee injury never healed properly and would plague him for the remainder of his life. To his death he blamed the riding instructor for permanently ruining his knee. Psychologically Eisenhower perceived his new handicap as a badge of shame that had cruelly changed the course of his life and negated any chance of his ever again playing sports. "I was like a man with his nose cut off going out into society!" he said.[41] He once tried running as a means of strengthening his knee but was dismayed to learn that it could not withstand the stress. The inevitable result was usually another dislocation. Eisenhower became so discouraged by a future without football and other sports that more than once he considered resigning, until common sense prevailed and he was talked out of it by his classmates. "Life seemed to have no meaning. A need to excel was gone," he lamented.[42] His entry in the 1915 *Howitzer* (the cadet yearbook), written by his roommate, cruelly lampooned that "Ike must content himself with tea, tiddleywinks and talk, at all of which he excels." His misery was evident when he wrote to Ruby Norman a few days after this setback that it seemed like "I am never cheerful anymore. The fellows that used to call me 'sunny jim' call me 'gloomy face' now. . . . I hate to be so worthless and helpless. . . . Anyway I'm getting to be such a confirmed grouch you'd hardly know me. Guess I'll come out of it soon though."[43]

Eisenhower managed to remain close to his beloved football team by becoming the head cheerleader in 1914–15. His experience leading pep rallies the night before games enhanced his ability to act and speak effectively in public. In addition, Coach Graves was so impressed with Eisenhower's grasp of football strategy that he encouraged him to take charge of the Cullum Hall junior varsity football team, which he did with considerable success. The high point of Eisenhower's four years at West Point occurred when he was presented the coveted letter *A* after the 1912 football season. "Ike was very nearly tickled to death," wrote P.A. "He hasn't received his sweater yet, though, and so can't wear it. He borrows mine occasionally so as to enjoy the sensation."[44]

Patton was never as good a football player as Eisenhower but both were relegated to intramural football during their plebe year. In 1905 Patton was likewise injured in a scrimmage against the varsity team, and hospitalized. He doggedly tried out each year for the football team but never earned the coveted *A* that was awarded to Eisenhower, even though he could no longer play. Eisenhower never lost his enthusiasm for the game. When Army beat Navy in 1913 he wrote exuberantly to Ruby Norman, "some game, some game! . . . the joy of the thing is too much—I feel my reason toppling."[45]

The injury had another equally serious consequence. With his morale and self-esteem at an all-time low, Eisenhower began a smoking habit that lasted until 1949. Although pipe and cigar smoking were permitted in cadet rooms, possession of cigarettes was a serious violation of West Point regulations—a fact that failed to dissuade Eisenhower or his classmates who had taken up the habit at the risk of expulsion. With cigarettes unavailable, those who dared to smoke rolled their own. Another bad habit begun at West Point was Eisenhower's practice of wolfing down his food so rapidly it was a wonder he even knew what he was eating. Notes Eisenhower scholar Robert H. Ferrell, "at first he did it for a reason, and later out of habit." To gain sufficient weight to make the football team, "he took up a crash regimen of eating everything in sight in the dining hall and ran his weight up twenty pounds." Both habits would later be of considerable medical concern.[46]

7.

"Popular but Undistinguished"

Poor Dwight merely consents to exist until graduation shall set him free.

—P. A. HODGSON

The impressive brick houses along West Point's faculty row have changed little since the early twentieth century. When once asked if he was ever invited by any of his instructors to their homes, Eisenhower replied derisively, "I didn't know any professors and I didn't want any of them to ask me in[to] their house, I'll tell you that." The cadets regarded both the faculty and the tactical department as the enemy. "We were thoroughly convinced," recalled Joseph Haw, "that the professors lay awake nights thinking up new ways to 'find' cadets deficient in studies and to ensure their departure from the sacred precincts of West Point."[1]

Although the class of 1915 was later dubbed "the class the stars fell on," the daring antics of some of its members made it a matter of astonishment that generals' stars ever fell on them. There was very little to do on weekends and even less for plebes. For diversion during Eisenhower's first year, two enterprising plebes inaugurated what they called "boxing smokers" in their room on alternate Saturday nights, when the upperclassmen were otherwise occupied at cadet hops. Entry required a spectator to "pay" his way in by fighting another cadet. It was inevitable that Eisenhower and Hodgson would be unable to resist the lure, and the two boxed each other as the price of admission. Friendship was momentarily forgotten. Paul was the quicker of the two, but Eisenhower's tactics were to savagely bore in and overwhelm his friend with a knockout punch.[2]

At West Point playing poker was another forbidden pastime that Eisenhower passionately embraced, usually when the tacs (army officers assigned to supervise the cadets) were the least vigilant. No one had money, and the stakes were pride. Having learned poker from a master, Eisenhower more than held his own. In 1913 he learned to play bridge, a game that would become his greatest source of entertainment for the rest of his life. As with everything Eisenhower did at West Point, he tempted disciplinary action by avidly playing after lights out.

Whenever Eisenhower and Hodgson were not otherwise engaged in breaking the rules, they kept their record intact by holding bull sessions after taps. A cadet would be detailed as a lookout to warn the group in the event a tac officer appeared. Eisenhower's penchant for talking elicited an entry in the 1915 yearbook, *Howitzer:*

INQUISITIVE CIVILIAN—Is Mr. Eisenhower good at athletics?
CAYDET—Yes, Mexican athletics.
INQUISITIVE CIVILIAN—What is that?
CAYDET—Slinging the bull.[3]

Dwight Eisenhower's passion for athletics was to have a profound effect on his choice of candidates to fill important roles during World War II. The sports-as-war metaphor was one that stuck with him. When it came to selecting the men who commanded major combat units in the European Theater of Operations, he rated athletes above others. To have excelled on the "friendly fields of strife," as MacArthur has said, was great preparation in Eisenhower's eyes. "I had occasion to be on the lookout for natural leaders. Athletes take a certain amount of kidding, especially from those who think it's always brain vs. brawn. But, I noted . . . how well ex-footballers seemed to have leadership qualifications and it wasn't sentiment that made it seem so."[4]

For the rest of his life he avidly followed the fortunes of the West Point football team. In 1960 President Eisenhower sent for the incoming superintendent, Lt. Gen. William C. Westmoreland. As their visit ended, Eisenhower pulled Westmoreland back into the Oval Office. "I do have one instruction for you, General," he said. "Do something about that damned football team," which had been faring badly of late.[5]

At the end of his plebe year Eisenhower's grades were respectable. His highest marks were in English, history, and military surveying; his worst subject was mathematics, in which he was rated 112th in the class. Neither Hodgson nor Eisenhower expected a promotion. "Dwight doesn't think he has any chance to get a 'corp' but I think he has," wrote P.A. to his mother. "He doesn't get as many demerits as I do, and he is fairly 'military' and thoroughly likeable."[6] Despite many unnecessary demerits and a less than sterling attitude, Eisenhower stood an acceptable thirty-ninth in conduct.[7] His record was good enough to earn him (and P.A.) a promotion to corporal, the highest rank a yearling could attain.

Most new upperclassmen took great pleasure in doling out the harassment they had received as plebes. Eisenhower was an exception and was never comfortable in the role of tormentor. In the summer of 1912 a plebe who happened to be from Kansas inadvertently bowled over Eisenhower, who arose and mocked the man by suggesting he looked like a barber. The plebe replied he had indeed been a barber in civilian life. The incident so embarrassed Eisenhower that he told P.A., "I'm never going to crawl another Plebe as long as I live. . . . I've done something that was stupid and unforgivable. I managed to make a man ashamed of the work he did for a living."[8]

After his third class (sophomore) year ended in June 1913, Eisenhower returned to Abilene as a newly promoted cadet supply sergeant for the ten weeks of his first and only summer furlough. Charlie Harger thought he detected a change in the young man, who seemed "more mature, more sedate. He felt the responsibility placed upon him. However, he was still the same high-spirited and attractive youth who had won the town's admiration in his boyhood days. He never showed the least touch of superiority in social activities."[9] Indeed, Eisenhower was now a small-town celebrity and the object of attention and admiration.

Harger's impressions differed significantly from those of Earl Eisenhower, who observed that in the summer of 1913 his older brother "was treated as the town hero, and he acted the part . . . [and] lost no opportunity to impress us with what he knew and had done." Eisenhower sometimes strutted around Abilene in his dress white summer uniform.[10] On one such occasion Eisenhower encountered Wes Merrifield, who was working in a local bakery. The two reminisced about their famous fight. For the first time Eisenhower publicly admitted that "I had the far worst of it. I'm willing to admit now that you really licked me then." A more mature person might have left it at that, but Eisenhower let his competitive nature get in the way of his common sense when he could not resist taking a parting shot at Merrifield. "But what I want to know," he challenged, "is whether you have any ambitions now." Merrifield had noted how Eisenhower had grown bigger and stronger during the years since their fight, and he judiciously replied, "Ike, I'm the most unambitious man in town."[11]

Unable to participate in summer sports, Eisenhower had to content himself with umpiring friendly baseball games between rival towns for fifteen dollars per game. Thanks to Bob Davis, he had had no trouble qualifying at West Point as a sharpshooter with a Springfield Model 1903 rifle. While killing time before the start of a game he was to umpire in a nearby town, Eisenhower stopped at a shooting gallery in his civilian clothes. Although no one knew him, he overheard a stranger offering to bet his friend ten dollars that Eisenhower would beat him. For the first time in his life he experienced sheer panic and began to tremble, his hands shaking. "Without a word, I laid down the rifle, having already paid for the shells, and left the place without a backward glance. Never before or since have I experienced the same kind of attack."[12]

An unfortunate incident marred an otherwise enjoyable furlough when

Eisenhower reluctantly fought a onetime professional fighter named Dirk Tyler, one of the few black men in mostly white Abilene. Tyler's modest success at fisticuffs had turned a well-regarded man into a local bully, who bragged that he had never been beaten by anyone in town. Eisenhower's reputation as a fighter led to an inevitable confrontation one day as he was getting a haircut in the barbershop where Tyler worked as a porter. Tyler none too subtly announced he was ready and willing to meet Ike "anywhere, anytime." Prodded by others and unable to resist this challenge to his manhood, Eisenhower reluctantly agreed to fight Tyler in the basement of a department store across the street.

Tyler was far superior in size and strength to Eisenhower, who instantly perceived that his only chance to whip his strapping opponent was to outbox him. Tyler's advantage was quickly nullified when he came out flailing punches, none of which troubled Eisenhower. Tyler consistently left his jaw unprotected, and the fight ended almost as soon as it began. Even with his injured knee, Eisenhower was the better boxer. Tyler was promptly flattened by a series of counterblows to the jaw and crumpled to the floor, out cold. "I went out determined to use every bit of skill to protect myself. And then to find that the boy didn't know the first thing about fighting! He telegraphed his punches from a mile away. Poor Dirk. Honestly, I've never been particularly proud of that scrap."[13]

At West Point token attempts were made to instill minimal social graces in the form of dancing classes and cadet hops, which had rigid rules of conduct. Eisenhower claims to have preferred poker to attending cadet hops, but his classmates remember him differently, as a "PSer"—which stood for "parlor snake," a term applied to anyone who loved to dance. The carefree Eisenhower was also often heard singing "Clementine" in the shower at the top of his lungs. His singing voice remained dreadfully off-key, and despite the pleas of his friends, such as cadet Mark Clark, who attempted to dissuade him, Eisenhower went through life blissfully butchering songs.[14]

During one of the occasions when he actually danced, Eisenhower was "skinned" for "improper dancing." "I guess her ankles showed or something," he later grumbled. "Dancing was very sedate at West Point in my days and we weren't very sedate."[15] In fact, Eisenhower was twice reported for the same infraction, the second time in June 1913 during a hop the night before his class departed on furlough. His partner, the daughter of a professor, asked him to dance the turkey trot, which he did with gusto. On his return to West Point in August 1913, he learned that a tactical officer had reported him. Since it was his second offense, Eisenhower was directed to appear before the commandant, who summarily reduced him to private, awarded eight demerits, confined Eisenhower to quarters for one month during off-duty time, and assessed twice-weekly punishment tours.[16]

It may well have been a record for the shortest time in grade before a newly promoted cadet was demoted. Later Eisenhower became one of seven members of the class on whom his classmates conferred the honorary title of "BA"—"busted aristocrat."

Throughout his West Point years Eisenhower remained extremely popular with his classmates, as much for his nonchalance as his sunny disposition. "There were some remarkable conversationalists in the class but the best of them had to talk fast to keep up with Ike. He could and did talk at the drop of a hat about anything, anytime, anywhere," said Haw. Eisenhower's academic indifference extended throughout his four years at West Point and failed "to impress the authorities with his fitness for appointment as a cadet officer. Despite his easy-going manner, no one doubted that his was an unusually strong character." During one of his numerous sojourns in the infirmary, a very sick cadet needed attention. "The soldier attendant made no move to comply with the cadet's urgent request. Standing on his good leg, Eisenhower told the orderly to hurry or he would 'knock hell out of him.' The man took one look at Ike's face and did the errand on the run."[17]

Eisenhower's strong influence on his devoted roommate was reflected during his absences in the infirmary. When he returned from yet another treatment of his ailing knee in 1913, P.A. wrote joyously to his mother, "Dwight came back to me yesterday and things seem much better already. Married life is a great thing for human contentment."[18]

For all his air of indifference, by his final year at West Point Eisenhower was already displaying traits of leadership. A classmate in confinement for taking an officer's horse on an unauthorized midnight ride was also a key member of the football team. Eisenhower was determined that the cadet be free to play against archenemy Navy. When he learned that the cadet was planning to break arrest to attend a hop, Eisenhower "came stalking in and told me that he'd smash a billiard cue over my head if I tried to break confinement. I stayed in quarters."[19]

Each cadet was usually required to recite at least once in each class on that day's assignment. They would first write the question or problem on the blackboard, then explain the answer when called on. Those unprepared were reported, and their only hope of avoiding trouble was to "bugle"—that is, stall in any way possible in the hope that the bugle call sounding the end of the class would come first. A cadet was called on in one of Eisenhower's classes without the foggiest notion of what he was doing. With five minutes left in the class, he was about to be "found" when his friend intervened. "Ike stood up and asked a question, then another, then still another. The instructor was completely taken in and answered each question thoroughly. Then the blessed bugle blew and I was off the hook. No 'bugler' was ever more expertly rescued."[20]

Eisenhower's stiffest challenge occurred during a class in integral calculus during his second year. A complex problem was presented that had to be solved the following day by one of the twelve cadets in the class. With the odds eleven to one that he would not be chosen, Eisenhower failed to prepare. As luck would have it, he was summoned to the blackboard to solve and explain the problem. Eisenhower remembers standing before the blackboard in a state of "mental paralysis" and "a sweat of helplessness." Facing severe disciplinary action and a poor grade if he failed, Eisenhower employed his math skills to devise a simpler, more logical solution. Instead of praising him, the instructor angrily accused him of memorizing the answer and of having written a meaningless series of numbers on the blackboard to deceive the class. Eisenhower stood his ground and vehemently rejected the assertion that he had cheated. "I gave one angry bark and I started a hot tirade."

About this time an associate professor of mathematics, Maj. J. Franklin Bell (affectionately nicknamed "Poopy"), quietly entered the classroom. Such inspections by a senior instructor were equated by the cadets with visitations from God. Ordering the instructor to have Eisenhower repeat his solution, Bell listened and then pronounced, "Mr. Eisenhower's solution is more logical and easier than the one we've been using. I'm surprised that none of us supposedly good mathematicians has stumbled on it. It will be incorporated in our procedures from now on." Eisenhower never forgot the debt he owed to "Poopy" Bell, or the fact that the instructor "was the only man I met at West Point for whom I ever developed any lasting resentment." Fifty-five years later Eisenhower wrote to thank Bell for saving his career that day. His bitterness about the slur upon his honesty was still unmistakable. "My army career could well have ended at that moment except for you. . . . I've always been certain that you saved me from making a spectacle of myself and getting tried for insubordination," he wrote, "for I was practically uncontrollable with anger."[21]

While at West Point, Eisenhower began to take a more active interest in members of the opposite sex. Women were naturally attracted to the handsome, gregarious, fun loving, and vain young man. His arrogance once landed him in a formidable social dilemma, when he tried to convince two young women that he was crazy about each of them. As his amused roommate wrote, "Unknown to him they were very good friends. . . . They then put their heads together and this week he received a pair of letters in which each volunteered to come up for the same dance." Somehow the crisis was averted, and "though [he is] rather wan and pale, his appetite is returning."[22]

During his senior year Eisenhower became intrigued with an attractive twenty-year-old Brooklynite named Dorothy Mills, who had been dating his roommate and was to be P.A.'s date for the graduation hop. His letters to Dorothy in 1914–15 begin to reveal another side to Eisenhower. For the most part the relationship never appeared to have serious overtones, and their correspondence was generally lighthearted. He eventually asked her to be his date for the annual Hundredth Night play. Dorothy was clearly attracted to Eisenhower but often offended by his flippant attitude, which only made him try harder to please her. His letters alternated from self-deprecating to pompously condescending. In reply to a particularly unseemly letter Dorothy once called him "a fresh masher."[23]

Eisenhower's letters to Dorothy Mills were small windows to a man no one ever really knew. In March there was an exchange of letters in which Dorothy wrote of their mutual "wanderlust." Eisenhower confessed: "It's affected me ever since I could walk. More than one night on furlough I spent all by my lonesome, out in the country—along the river bank—or up in the hills—just walking—smoking and . . . as I think of it—this is the first time I've told it. But one morning, I got in town just as a girl I knew was going up to take an early train. . . . She asked me later where I'd been—but I never tried to explain . . . she'd have suspected me of being 'touched'—or at least possessed of a sickly sentimentalism—which is worse."[25]

Sentimentality was a trait Eisenhower eschewed. Throughout his life he rarely displayed his true feelings to his family or his associates. Whatever he felt deeply was mostly a mystery he was loath to permit anyone to unlock. From time to time he permitted the briefest of glimpses before the door slammed shut and he again assumed the role of stern father and ever-efficient career soldier. Like most men of his generation, Eisenhower deemed it unmanly to unburden himself. His son, John, would later write of his father's remoteness, "Dad was a terrifying figure to a small boy."[26]

For all his gregariousness, Eisenhower was a solitary man. When not showing off the side of his personality he wanted the world to see, Eisenhower found solace by himself, often on the steep banks overlooking the Hudson River, in what Kenneth Davis has called "his secret life." Whenever the demands of the strict regimen permitted, Eisenhower liked nothing better than to explore the wilds of the West Point reservation and its steep cliffs above the river. Sometimes he stopped in the ruins of Fort Putnam, which formed the bulwark of the American defense of the Hudson during the Revolutionary War. Here, unburdened and undistracted by cadet duties, he would critique the battles, assess the terrain as a military commander would have, and re-create in his mind how they were fought and what mistakes were made by both sides. "As laboratory studies he considered them a major factor in his education as a cadet."[27]

Another glimpse of the stubborn Eisenhower can be seen in a letter P. A. Hodgson wrote to his parents in March 1912, the year former president Theodore Roosevelt ran in a three-way race for the presidency, against the incumbent Republican, William Howard Taft, and his Democratic challenger, Woodrow Wilson. Roosevelt had bolted the Republican Party to form his own Progressive "Bull Moose" ticket, and his espousal of neutrality toward Europe so angered Eisenhower that Hodgson thought him unreasonably stubborn. For reasons that never made sense to P.A., Eisenhower suddenly developed an intense dislike for his boyhood hero. "I never knew any one with such a strong and at the same time, causeless and unreasonable dislike for another, as he has for Roosevelt," wrote Hodgson. "You'd think that Teddy had done him some irreparable wrong from the way he talks and he hasn't a reason in the world for his attitude. He actually offered to bet me his furlough that Roosevelt wouldn't even be nominated."[28]

For all his casual attitude toward West Point, by early in his third year he would write to Ruby, "Remember that it is good to write once in a while, just to keep in practice—also that West Point, N.Y. looks awfully nice as an address on an envelope."[29] His letters also began to exhibit the first signs of sexual awareness and innuendo. In November 1913, for example, Eisenhower wrote that if Ruby's six-person all-girl orchestra was in New York during his Christmas leave, "we don't know *what might* happen. . . . I'm not going to open up and tell you all I'd really like to this evening. . . . I've changed my views concerning matrimony. I saw in the paper it was 'kisstomary to cuss the bride' so me for it. I'm looking for someone that I can pummel and bruise and pinch and fight and etc etc."[30]

One of Eisenhower's surviving letters was to a young lady named Brush, whom he had met at the 1914 Army-Navy football game, in which P.A. starred for Army in one of their greatest victories over the midshipmen of Annapolis. "It was a great day and a greater game. The only thing I regretted was that I couldn't inflict my presence on that delightful party after the game—but fate, the hussy interfered." His letter continued, "Just a second, my skag [cigarette] went out—All lit up once more. The whole purpose of this letter was to ask you to write me, and since I got up the courage to do it, I reckon I'd better stop . . . what do you think of Hodgson, the man that made that long run at the beginning of the game. Some boy, and he's my 'roomie.' I'm some proud! . . . in case you've forgotten my name, it is, D. D. Eisenhower."[31]

Newspapers and radios were a rarity at West Point, but Eisenhower and P.A. nevertheless managed to track on a map the events transpiring in Europe after World War I erupted in 1914. They put pins in the map to denote the movement of the opposing armies, a practice Eisenhower had begun in Abilene in 1904 during the Russo-Japanese War, and would employ the rest of his military career. During their senior year, Eisenhower and his classmates also traveled to Gettysburg, where they spent three days studying the most important battle of the Civil War.

Near the end of his junior year Eisenhower inscribed a permanent reminder of his presence at West Point by etching "Ike Eisenhower" on the copper sheathing of a corner of the inside roof of the cadet chapel.

In his first class (senior) year in 1914–15, he was promoted to F Company color sergeant. Although he continued to rack up demerits, this time Eisenhower managed to hang on to his sergeant's stripes. His first sergeant was his close friend, a mild-mannered, soft-spoken young man, with a pronounced Missouri accent, Omar N. Bradley. Their friendship was based on their rural Midwest roots and a passionate love of sports. Bradley played baseball and was known as an outfielder with a strong arm and a high batting average. After several earlier tryouts, Bradley also made the varsity football team in 1914, playing in five games, and later reflected that, "No extracurricular endeavor I know of could better prepare a soldier for the battlefield."[32]

Bradley's somber face and hangdog looks resulted in the cruel designation of "ugliest man in his class." Eisenhower, who had long since learned the folly of personal insults, was outraged when a classmate once likened Bradley to an ape. Next to sports, Bradley's other consuming passion was F Company, and he earned considerable prestige for refusing a promotion that would have meant a transfer to another company. "Sir, I would rather be first sergeant of "F" Co. than captain of any other company," he declared.[33]

Whenever football was involved Eisenhower's attitude changed dramatically. As the assistant coach of the Cullum Hall football team in 1914, Eisenhower both impressed and inspired his players by his hard work and dedication, which may well have been one of the first manifestations of his emerging leadership skills. He also joined the West Point chapter of the YMCA, which met every Sunday evening to hear a different speaker. The principal function of the YMCA was Bible study. Its members also helped teach Sunday school to the children of West Point personnel. Eisenhower quietly taught one of the classes.[34]

As graduation approached in the spring of 1915, Eisenhower's unresolved knee injury was deemed sufficiently serious that the army planned to deny him a commission. According to a classmate, a medical board had already decided that Eisenhower was physically unfit. Had it not been for the timely intervention of a white knight in the person of the academy surgeon, Lt. Col. Henry A. Shaw, Cadet Eisenhower would not have been commissioned in June 1915. Fortunately Shaw was a pragmatist who believed that neither Eisenhower nor the army would benefit by such a decision. He lobbied members of the tactical department and the academic board to support Eisenhower. Shaw's efforts paid off when the decision was reversed and the War Department agreed.[35]

Shaw summoned Eisenhower and offered to recommend his commissioning if he would apply for the coast artillery. Eisenhower knew the coast artillery to be a dead-end career in a service that, in his opinion, "provided a numbing series of routine chores and a minimum of excitement" and, to Shaw's annoyance, instantly spurned the proposition. Given that Shaw himself had served in the coast artillery, Eisenhower's disdainful rejection could have proved fatal. The young man who would one day become renowned for his tactfulness as a supreme commander was especially fortunate to have had a forgiving officer like Shaw on his side. Eisenhower shrugged it off, declaring that if he could not serve in the U.S. Army he would pack up, move to Argentina (a place he had learned about in his study of geography), and become a gaucho. He even sent for travel literature before abandoning the idea.

Several days later Eisenhower was summoned again by Shaw. "He said he realized that [a] great part of the injury was [horseback] riding. . . . So he said, 'Mr. Eisenhower, if you will not ask for a mounted service, I will recommend you for commission.' " Eisenhower readily agreed, noting that his preference was the infantry. Shaw, he said, concurred, and according to Eisenhower, the three choices entered on his preference sheet were identical: "Infantry." His official personnel file for 1915, however, records that the commandant of cadets noted his preferences as: (1) infantry, (2) coast artillery, and (3) cavalry. To everyone's relief he was accepted in the infantry.[36]

Eisenhower's recurring four-year affiliation with the post infirmary nearly caused him to miss his own graduation. He was admitted for the last time on June 6, 1915, with acute influenza.[37] By the time he graduated several days later, it had practically verged on the miraculous that Eisenhower somehow managed to avoid being expelled from West Point. Whereas Cadet Patton would agonize over demerits and attempt to deport himself as perfectly as possible in everything he did, Cadet Eisenhower became noted as a fun-loving maverick who would not back down when he believed himself in the right, no matter who in authority demanded it. The parallels between the two at West Point are almost eerily similar. Both young men were obsessive in their desire to succeed in athletics. Patton had to repeat his plebe year after failing a mathematics exam in 1905, and his undiagnosed dyslexia dogged him throughout his five years there.

Each considered quitting. While Eisenhower spoke of going to Argentina to become a gaucho if he was not commissioned, Lt. Patton unsuccessfully attempted to participate in World War I before the United States entered the war. He begged for a leave of absence to accept a commission in the French army but was turned down.[38] The escalating troubles with Mexico in 1913 led both young men to anticipate the coming conflict with relish. In Pattonesque language Eisenhower wrote to Ruby Norman, "The only bright spot is, just now, that trouble with Mexico seems imminent. We may stir up a little excitement yet, let's hope so, at least."[39]

The graduation address was delivered on June 12, 1915, by President Woodrow Wilson's secretary of war, Lindley M. Garrison, whose brief speech contained the usual exhortations to excel and sacrifice, and was immediately forgotten by most. Afterward the new graduates swore to uphold and defend the Constitution and were duly commissioned as second lieutenants in the U.S. Army. That night the men of the class of 1915 attended a gala graduation dinner held at New York's prestigious Astor Hotel, followed by attendance at a hit Broadway musical.

Eisenhower was easily the youngest-looking graduate of the class of 1915 and certainly one of the most popular. Although generally humorous, Eisenhower's entry in the *Howitzer* by P. A. Hodgson was regarded by some classmates as being in poor taste. Although it was traditional to lampoon one another, "Ike" was described as "the terrible Swedish-Jew, as big as life and twice as natural. He claims to have the best authority for the statement that he is the handsomest man in the Corps. . . . Poor Dwight merely consents to exist until graduation shall set him free. . . . [He] won his 'A' by being the most promising back in Eastern football—but the Tufts game broke his knee and the promise."[40]

Bradley's entry in the 1915 *Howitzer* was written by Eisenhower and would prove remarkably prophetic. "His most prominent characteristic," he wrote, " 'is getting there,' and if he keeps up the clip he's started, some of us will one some day be bragging to our grandchildren that 'sure, General Bradley was a classmate of mine.' "

The extent to which Eisenhower took West Point seriously until after his graduation is debatable. Beyond attaining a coveted all-expenses-paid college education (and indulging his passion for sports), he had yet to display any great commitment to becoming an army officer for the next eight years, the time then required for all graduates to serve on active duty. Moreover, not everyone was impressed. Later assessments by two officers who served in the tactical department were wildly dissimilar. One rated him "Born to command," while another said, "We saw in Eisenhower a not uncommon type, a man who would thoroughly enjoy his Army life, giving both to duty and recreation their fair values. We did not see in him a man who would throw himself into his job so completely that nothing else would matter." The commandant of cadets noted in an official evaluation that Eisenhower "should be assigned to an organization under [a] strict commanding officer."[41]

Yet, for all his alleged indifference, Eisenhower had learned far more than his deportment revealed about his preparation to assume the duties and responsibilities of an officer. Academically he did far better than his recollections suggest, graduating 61 of 164. Not surprisingly, however, he stood 125th in discipline. His eagerness to move on was reflected in his disciplinary record in 1914–15, during which he earned 100 demerits, the most of his four-year tenure at West Point.

For most graduates the West Point experience evokes mixed feelings. Not so Dwight Eisenhower. "I enjoyed West Point; I was one of the few that really thought I was having a good time . . . getting an education when you don't have to pay for it when I'd been working for two years to help my brother? Well, I thought this was a wonderful thing. I absorbed West Point and I think no cadet was more jealous of its reputation and its honor system. But I just wasn't bothered about the little things."[42]

His official biographer has noted how Eisenhower had "drifted" through West Point just as he had in Abilene, but correctly surmised that he "took from West Point what was positive and rejected that which was negative."[43] Still, it remained a measure of Eisenhower's immaturity that he so often and so frivolously risked losing the very education and opportunities he had dedicated himself to obtaining.

For all their hardships, both Eisenhower and Douglas MacArthur were typical of so many graduates whose veneration of West Point lasted a lifetime. Joseph Haw may well have spoken for the class of 1915 when he noted that "the historic traditions of West Point were rarely discussed yet somehow the part of the academy had played in the history of our country was unconsciously absorbed by the most thoughtless cadet. . . . There was no flag-waving but there grew up within us a deep pride in our school and our army and a feeling that we must live up to the great tradition we had inherited."[44]

The roster of the class of 1915 would later read like a military who's who of World War II. They ranged from his Missouri friend, the soft-spoken Bradley, to Joseph Swing and future U.S. Air Force general George Stratemeyer. James Van Fleet and Joseph McNarney would attain four-star rank. Seven others would reach the three-star rank of lieutenant general, twenty-four became major generals (fifteen of whom commanded divisions in combat), and twenty-five brigadier generals. All told more than half the 115 graduates who served in World War II became generals. No West Point class before or since has produced so many—two of whom, Bradley and Eisenhower, rose to the five-star rank of general of the army—and one, Dwight Eisenhower, also became the thirty-fourth president of the United States. To this day "the class the stars fell on" remains the most famous in West Point history.

For all his compliments about West Point, Eisenhower's remembrance of his four years was mixed. "I wanted no part of that," he said, after refusing to consider seriously an offer to become commandant of cadets in 1937. Nor was Eisenhower the first to deprecate his West Point experience to conceal his true feelings, which grew deeper with age. One of his oldest friends, Gen. Mark Clark, visited a gravely ill Eisenhower frequently before his death in 1969 in Walter Reed Army Hospital. "But you know, all he wanted to talk about was West Point. Not about being president, not about being supreme commander, about D-Day, none of that. West Point was all, ever."[45]

With tongue in cheek, the editors of the *Howitzer* captioned a photograph of the cadet barracks, "Wherein reside the nation's pampered pets." The last entry in the 1915 *Howitzer* was a photograph of a cadet with the caption "Lights Out." The same could be said for Eisenhower's West Point years. Ahead of him lay the long train journey back to Abilene and the uncertainty of learning a new profession in a minuscule peacetime army as a newly commissioned second lieutenant of infantry.

8.

"1915—the Summer Dwight Came Back from West Point"

I love you Gladys.

When Eisenhower returned to Abilene in June 1915, Ida presented him with a copy of the standard version of the Bible used by the Jehovah's Witnesses.[1] The book became a treasured keepsake on which Eisenhower later swore the oath of office when he was inaugurated as president in January 1953.

Although eligible to draw the pay of a second lieutenant, Eisenhower was in temporary limbo. His commission was not official until formally signed by the president. Typically commissions were signed promptly, but Woodrow Wilson was otherwise absorbed not only with the outbreak of World War I in Europe but with the escalating lawlessness along the Mexican border. Before the commission could be formalized, the adjutant general sent Eisenhower two forms to complete. One asked for his place of birth, to which he inexplicably entered "Tyler, Texas." As late as 1963 the uncertainty over Eisenhower's birthplace was still a subject of misunderstanding. Based on conversations with his father, John Eisenhower wrote to a Dallas newsman that his father "believed his birthplace to be Tyler for many years." However, there was no logical reason for the slightest confusion in Eisenhower's mind. At West Point in 1911, and subsequently on forms that asked for "Candidate's Place of Birth," Eisenhower unfailingly entered "Denison, Texas."[2]

Eisenhower spent the summer of 1915 vowing "to have a good time" during what turned out to be the most bittersweet interlude of his life. Although he was regularly "slugged" (another term coined by cadets for a violation of Academy regulations resulting in dements) at West Point for a variety of uniform violations, when he was home in Abilene, Eisenhower suddenly became utterly fastidious in his dress. During his summer leave in 1913 one of the reasons he had often worn his cadet uniform around town was to impress not only the townsfolk but a young woman on whom he had a secret crush while attending Abilene High School. She was Gladys Harding, the blue-eyed, blond daughter of a successful Abilene businessman, an accomplished pianist, and reputed to have been one of the prettiest girls in town. Although the two had been friends throughout high school, their relationship never passed beyond mutual admiration until the summer of 1913, when Eisenhower finally dared to ask Gladys for a date. She readily accepted, and despite the existence of other would-be beaux (as befitted one of Abilene's prettiest girls), they not only dated frequently but the first signs of a more serious romance took root.

Suddenly Eisenhower began spending most evenings in her company at the nearby Harding home, often wearing his uniform to impress Gladys and her father. The ritual beforehand was excruciating. Ida was recruited to carefully iron his uniform pants, which, her son informed her, "have to be so well pressed that they will stand up by themselves." Milton and Earl did the rest, acting as aides-de-camp. "Dwight lay on the bed while we eased his razor-sharp trousers on, one leg at a time. Then he stood up slowly, so as not to spoil the crease."[3]

Before returning to West Point in 1913, Eisenhower asked Six McDonnell to watch over Gladys while he was gone and "take her to a show once in a while." McDonnell complied but became infatuated with Gladys. He dated her a number of times and once obtained leave from his baseball team, then playing in Nebraska, to pay a surprise visit to Abilene to see Gladys, even hiring a taxi for the final leg of the trip. Six intended to be dropped off at the Harding house until he spied Gladys and Eisenhower in his cadet uniform sitting in chairs on the lawn. Instead he hastily told the taxi driver to " 'Just keep on going.' The next morning I went back to Lincoln. . . . I was embarrassed."[4]

Eisenhower and Gladys were briefly reunited in December 1914, when the traveling Apollo Concert Company, in which she did recitals and pianologues, played in New York City. He savored his classmates' envy that such an attractive woman was his date. Although none of the Eisenhower family attended his graduation from West Point, held in June, his only regret seems to have been his disappointment that Gladys was unable to be present.

In the summer of 1915 their budding romance was revived when Gladys was on summer hiatus. The two became virtually inseparable, with most of their evenings together spent in the Harding home, much to Mr. Harding's growing dismay over his daughter's romance with Eisenhower. Not unreasonably, he was convinced that she had no future married to a soldier with no money and few prospects, and urged Gladys to ditch him. "That Eisenhower kid will never amount to anything," he predicted.[5] As children are wont to do, Gladys ignored her father's exhortations.

Although he and Gladys were soon seeing each other on a daily basis, Eisenhower felt compelled to write her love letters, which he delivered personally. They vividly expressed the amorous feelings of a young man in love for the first time. In one he declared his "need and hunger for you," and deemed himself "far luckier than I ever even dared hope . . . your soldier boy really *loves* you." Eisenhower's words left no doubt of his intentions. He found in Gladys "the purest, sweetest and strongest love he ever gave to a woman except his mother, and loved you as a man does the one woman, whom in his most cherished dreams, he hopes some day to call his wife."

When they were not together, Gladys was noting her own growing feelings. She kept Eisenhower's letters, and in an intimate diary recorded the progress of their romance, which she called, "1915—The Summer Dwight Came Back from West Point." The extent of her love for Eisenhower is quite evident in a cover note she wrote in 1957: "Letters—from Dwight D. Eisenhower—that I rec'd, when we were *young* and *happy*! (Back in 1914–1915)."[6]

On August 5 Gladys wrote in her diary, "D. asked me to marry him." She neither accepted nor rejected Eisenhower's proposal, and although clearly torn, was simply not prepared to commit herself to a marriage that would effectively end her musical career. Nor could her father's attitude have helped, an obstacle likewise encountered by Patton during his courtship of his future wife, Beatrice Ayer. The U.S. Army was widely thought to be a dead-end career that paid slave wages to men otherwise regarded as the misfits of society. Patton's future father-in-law, the self-made millionaire tycoon Frederick Ayer, possessed "the typical New England view of the 'brutal and licentious mercenary.' . . . the Yankee[s] always thought of the army as the refuge for thieves and murderers."[7] No doubt Mr. Harding held a similar view.

With little else to do in Abilene, whenever he was not in Gladys's company, Eisenhower could usually be found hunting, fishing, and occasionally drinking or playing poker. One evening he and several friends had imbibed enough bootleg whiskey to become loud and boisterous when they ambled into a local café. Eisenhower attempted to teach his friends some of his West Point songs in his dreadful singing voice, which, more often than not, resulted in exhortations that he *please* stop. Eisenhower defied several profane requests from the owner to stop or be tossed out, responding by angrily daring him to try; then, to make the point, he thrust his fist through the wall of the café, where it became stuck. A portion of the wall had to be cut away with a kitchen knife to free a very chagrined Dwight Eisenhower. Although he later characterized the incident as "wildly exaggerated," it was nevertheless a vivid illustration that after four years at West Point, Eisenhower was still unable to control his explosive temper.[8] It was a side of his personality that Gladys Harding never glimpsed.

In September, Gladys was set to return to her touring company, and Dwight thought he would soon be leaving for the Philippines. As their time together grew ever shorter, Eisenhower's penchant for keeping a tight rein on his emotions failed him. In the early morning hours of August 17, 1915, he penned the first of the two most impassioned letters of his life. "Dearest Girl," he wrote:

> . . . I think I appreciate you more than ever before. I have a keener realization of your worth and sweetness—and feel how lucky I am that you give me even a thought. . . . More than ever, now, I want to hear you say the three words with "Better than I ever have anyone in the world!" If you can say that to me . . . then I'll know that I've *won*. From that time—if it ever comes—I'll know you're mine—no matter where you go—or what you do. . . . For girl I do love you and want you to KNOW it—to be as certain of it as I am—and to believe in me and trust me as you would your dad. . . .
>
> Sept 1st seems so fearfully close . . . this parting is going to be the hardest so far in my life. . . . I don't know how little or how much you do love me—but I do know that you do not care now like I dare to hope that you will.
>
> Please don't think that I'm presuming to be worthy of even the faintest spark of affection from you. I know that I've made miserable mistakes and botches—but girl I'm *trying*. . . .

Decked out in his white dress uniform, Eisenhower accompanied Gladys to Kansas City, where she boarded a train for New York on September 1. Their final three days together were poignant. In her diary Gladys wrote, "Sad parting. **** Love *." Her only visual memories of Eisenhower were his name card from his graduation hop at West Point, "a faded red rose and the remnants of a four-leaf clover."[9]

After their farewell a heartbroken and by now rather desperate Eisenhower endured a fitful night in a Kansas City hotel where he poured out his pent-up feelings in a letter addressed to "Sweet girl of Mine." "My heart seems to choke me," he wrote. "And yet there is a certain happiness there too. Even while seeing you go—I know that you love me—me! And, oh girl! that knowledge is the great and wondrous influence which will help me through this coming year and bring me to you again—to claim you forever and always and now sweetheart good night. Your devoted Dwight."

Gladys replied at once from New York, prompting yet another declaration of Eisenhower's love. Calling her "his beautiful lady," he wrote that he simply had to "just whisper over and over 'I love you Gladys'—'I love you Gladys' . . . I'll meet you in Dreamland—if you will meet me there. And *there*—as sometime in reality—you *shall* be my dearest and closest friend—my own sweetheart and true blue wife."[10]

Eisenhower's letters may have been mushy, even mawkish, but there is no doubt of his love for Gladys Harding in the summer of 1915. However, unlike so many summer romances, this one, in hindsight, might well have survived had Eisenhower not met his future wife soon after reporting for duty at Fort Sam Houston. Although the two exchanged letters for a time, and both continued to profess their love, their geographical separation began to cool the romance. Subsequent events have revealed that Gladys Harding was very much in love with Dwight Eisenhower and fully expected him to marry her. Six McDonnell likewise thought Eisenhower and Gladys would marry, and was surprised when they did not.[11]

Whatever misgivings either had over their breakup in September 1915 were taken to the grave. Eisenhower never publicly or privately mentioned his first serious romance. Still, the two never forgot each other. They exchanged infrequent, innocuous letters until Gladys's death in 1959, but neither ever again spoke about the summer of 1915. When President Eisenhower visited Abilene in 1953, the most exciting incident of his visit occurred when "a plump woman with blond hair darted out into the street and bore down on his motorcade." The president's Secret Service escorts began reacting to this apparent threat but even after thirty-eight years Dwight Eisenhower recognized his old flame. He ordered the driver to stop, and to the delight of the crowd the two embraced; then Eisenhower "gave her a hearty kiss." His obvious affection for this woman from his past "made Mamie madder than hell," remembered Earl Endacott.[12]

The only other woman close to Eisenhower was Ruby Norman, who always insisted that her relations with Ike were strictly platonic. "I was his friend. Gladys Harding was his *girl*. She was the only girl he ever had in Abilene."[13]

In early August 1915, Eisenhower's commission arrived, and he wrote at once to the adjutant general that, "I accept the commission as Second Lieutenant of Infantry."[14] His preference sheet listed the Philippines, a remote posting that, despite its hardships, offered adventure and possible combat. In the past, duty in the Philippines was considered a rather routine assignment for a newly commissioned officer. And, as the only cadet in his class to request such duty, Eisenhower was so confident of a Philippine assignment that he purchased only tropical uniforms, but none of the other types required for service elsewhere. What he had not counted on was that the problems with Mexico resulted in Regular Army troops being sent to guard the border from California to Brownsville, Texas. Although there was as yet no actual state of war between the Mexico and the United States, border duty was so miserable that the War Department began receiving numerous requests for Philippine duty, which had suddenly became a far more attractive alternative.

At West Point between $14 and $15 had been withheld from his pay every month until graduation, when Eisenhower received what seemed to him a financial windfall. The amount left over from his partial uniform purchases was used to finance his summer vacation in Abilene. Oblivious to the fact that the War Department might not approve his request, Eisenhower was embarrassed to learn he would be traveling only as far as Fort Sam Houston, in San Antonio, Texas. His savings soon ran out, and to continue his courtship of Gladys Harding, Eisenhower was obliged to borrow from his father merely to make it through the summer.[15] He also hocked his watch to Earl for a small loan that was never repaid.

The announcement of his new assignment required Eisenhower to report to Fort Sam Houston in mid-September, with all mandatory uniforms in his possession, for duty with the 19th Infantry Regiment. In desperation he visited a well-known uniform outfitter in Leavenworth and purchased his uniforms on credit. On a second lieutenant's minuscule pay of $141.67 per month, Eisenhower was already well in debt before ever serving a single day on active duty.[16] It was an inauspicious beginning to his military career.

9.

Miss Mamie Doud

I made up my mind, I was going to make myself as good an Army officer as I could.

The young man who graduated from West Point in 1915 was to become as much of an enigma as Patton, who in a few short years would become one of his closest friends. The image Dwight Eisenhower presented to the world was vastly different from the inner man. Eisenhower's future brilliance was masked by the extroverted personality of an underachiever with a perpetual demeanor of casual rebelliousness and nonchalance. Publicly he remained seemingly without a care in the world and determined to sample life's pleasures while in the service of the U.S. Army.

So much for the facade. Behind his genuine love of his hometown and his sunny smile lay Eisenhower's lifelong fear of being regarded as a country bumpkin. As one observer has astutely noted, "All his life, believing it a weakness, he would disguise the great country within him, giving his mother's friendliness to the public world and his father's toughness to the practical problems of command. They were studied roles, both of them, calculated to misdirect. He feared nothing so much as exposure."[1]

Unlike the public person he later became, Eisenhower studiously shunned the limelight whenever possible. In San Antonio he once attended a victory dance at a local hotel to celebrate the triumphant 1915 football season of Saint Louis College, a tiny Catholic school that Eisenhower had coached to its first victories in five years. When he entered the ballroom, "Everybody stopped and started clapping and cheering. I blushed like a baby—Gee! surely was embarrased [*sic*]. I made a run for a corner, believe me."[2]

Those who mistook Dwight Eisenhower for nothing more than a country boy never saw the depth of intelligence behind the charm and the smile. "No one seems to have understood that he was a brilliant man. He was not an intellectual, and perhaps that fact confused people of intellect who assume intelligence must always breathe an air of the salon."[3] This outgoing persona would be his armor against the slings and arrows of the uncertain world he now entered.

Eisenhower had no illusions about his future in the army, believing it unthinkable that he could ever earn a general's stars in peacetime. He also went to great lengths to assume the role he had decided to carve out for himself: that of a solid, dependable officer who performed his duties efficiently but without drawing undue attention to himself. "I wasn't too concerned about promotion . . . and when my son John wanted to go to West Point I told him never to think about promotion but to do his job well and make every boss sorry when he leaves."[4]

Eisenhower Spartan explanation was part of the deception. Two of the most competitive soldiers in the U.S. Army were Dwight Eisenhower and George S. Patton. Though it was never evident in public, Dwight Eisenhower simply hated to lose or be crossed. As a previous biographer has noted, he was not spiteful but neither was he particularly forgiving, even with lifelong friends whose actions displeased him. John Eisenhower experienced firsthand his father's ultracompetitive nature. "Dad could get over any disagreement very easily, as long as he won."[5] A senior officer always walks on the right, and his subordinates on the left. As a boy, and later an army officer, John learned never to violate this army custom. For those who knew Eisenhower or worked for him, his temper was as notorious as his grin was famous. Whatever David Eisenhower and his son Dwight had in common did not extend to the father's abhorrence of swearing, alcohol in any form, smoking, gambling, or card playing. By the time Dwight graduated from West Point and became an army officer, he had done all of them.[6]

The military establishment of which Eisenhower became a part in 1915 was ingrained with the view that the military as an established institution was apolitical and conservative in outlook. He entered the army at a time when "The new American professional officer had an inbred respect for the integrity of the chain of command," as Samuel P. Huntington wrote in his landmark study, *The Soldier and the State*. The president of the United States was deemed a benevolent figure of respect and admiration to whom each officer owed his unqualified allegiance as commander in chief of the armed forces. "Duty is the Army's highest law . . . ," noted Huntington. "The twenty years prior to World War I were the heyday of the belief that war might be prevented by treaties or institutional devices. Again and again the military warned that Peace Palaces would not bring peace."[7] (This peace principle was the very foundation of Woodrow Wilson's presidency and would prove as fragile as it was misguided.)

In addition to a reverence for the presidency, West Point had also repeatedly instilled in young Eisenhower and his classmates a thorough distrust of politics and politicians. The cadets were inculcated with, and readily came to accept, the premise that politicians in general, and Congress in particular, were a contemptible, dishonest lot. During the 1930s, when Eisenhower spent nearly five years toiling in the War Department, his aversion to politicians would harden. As a body the officer corps avoided politics to the point where fewer than one in five hundred ever bothered to register as a member of a political party or vote in an election. The still-vivid historical example of Grant's disastrous presidency served as a clear affirmation that the military and politics simply did not mix. While it held relatively little importance in the performance of his duties as a junior officer, this belief would later have enormous implications in Eisenhower's performance as supreme commander.

During the summer of 1915 Eisenhower decided the time had come for him to change his blasé attitude. "I made up my mind," he said, that henceforth "I was going to make myself as good an Army officer as I could. Out of whatever I could do, it wasn't going to be a lack of work that kept me from doing it. I worked very hard. Now, I had my fun, and a lot of fun, but I did work very hard."[8] Notes Stephen Ambrose, "It was resolve rather than an ambition, and sprang from a sense of obligation and responsibility rather than from a competitive drive, for he felt that with the end of his sports career, his competitive days were over."[9]

In the summer of 1915 American troubles with Mexico had escalated to the point where Eisenhower's regiment was ordered to border duty in Galveston. Eisenhower arrived in Galveston in mid-September only to learn that the 19th Infantry Regiment had been flooded out of its cantonment and had returned to Fort Sam Houston. He took the next train to San Antonio and reported for duty. He was assigned to Company F, commanded by Capt. George W. Helms, whom Eisenhower would later recall with fondness. "I shall never forget the day I reported to you. . . . Because I had some little reputation as a football player, you were apparently expecting a regular Goliath, and expressed your immediate disappointment that I was a man of medium build and size." Helms's tolerance toward his new lieutenant was reciprocated when he took "charge of my somewhat unruly, harum-scarum personality in time to keep me from getting too far off the track. I owe a lot to you personally; a fact which I never forgot."[10]

The small standing Regular Army of 1915 was poorly paid and its enlisted ranks populated by men of scant education and little ambition. Between 1895—when the figure was less than $52 million—and 1916, the average military budget was barely $150 million, and funds to improve the squalid living conditions in the army's remote outposts were virtually nonexistent.[11] The active army in 1915 totaled 106,754 (4,948 officers and 101,806 enlisted men), most of whom were dispersed in small military garrisons that were rarely larger than battalion size. These tiny outposts were a relic of eighteenth-century frontier America. Unlike that of Wilson, Theodore Roosevelt's administration believed that the U.S. Army must be modernized to fight a future war but had run afoul of politicians determined to retain the status quo and the "fort" mentality.[12] Until U.S. entry into World War I in 1917, Wilson had evinced little interest in the military, and during his first administration the military continued to stagnate.

There was no better example of the boredom of military life than the high desertion rate and the high occupancy rate of the post stockade. Drunkenness remained a serious problem and in many places, particularly the larger cities, enlisted men were regarded with utter contempt. Discipline was swift and harsh, the duty usually mind numbing, and the pay—though better in the U.S. Army than in other armies—wretchedly low. Some enlisted without fully understanding what they were letting themselves in for; literacy was a major problem, and conditions, albeit improved from those of the post–Civil War period, were at best austere. Life was governed by the call of the bugle.

An exception was Fort Sam Houston, one of the crown jewels of the prewar army. With its lovely brick quarters, famous quadrangle, and easygoing ambiance, it was one of the most popular and sought-after assignments for an officer. Except, that is, Dwight Eisenhower, whose hopes of a Philippine assignment had been abruptly dashed.

Peacetime duty at one of the army's prestigious military posts hardly posed a challenge. Fort Sam Houston had been a military post since 1845, the year Texas joined the Union. Originally called the "Post of San Antonio," it was renamed in 1890 in honor of the father of Texas. Opportunities abounded for participation in social life. So many officers were married there that Fort Sam (as it was informally called) eventually earned the nickname the "mother-in-law" of the army. The pace was generally unhurried, with as much time available for sports and socializing as for military duties.

As the newest arrival, Eisenhower automatically earned the dubious distinction of being the most junior second lieutenant in the regiment. He was assigned to regimental duties suitable for a junior officer. The regimental commander, Col. Millard Fillmore Waltz, an 1879 graduate of West Point, had served with distinction on the western frontier and in the Spanish-American War. A tough, bad-tempered, no-nonsense Regular Army infantry officer who suffered neither fools nor second lieutenants gladly, his bull-like demeanor so thoroughly intimidated his junior officers that they made it a point to avoid him whenever possible. Other than formally reporting to his new commanding officer in September, Eisenhower had yet to make the acquaintance of Colonel Waltz.

With little disposable income for recreation, Eisenhower and his fellow bachelor lieutenants were a restless lot and spent a great deal of their free time wandering aimlessly around Fort Sam in search of entertainment. Almost anything would do. One evening, in a most unmilitary fashion, Eisenhower and some other lieutenants were lingering near the fifty-foot-high post flagpole, which was anchored by steel cables. Eisenhower bragged that having done considerable rope climbing at West Point, he could easily scale one of the support cables to the top, using only his hands. His challenge was so utterly disparaged that one officer offered to bet the not insignificant sum of five dollars that Eisenhower would fail.

Sensing quick compensation for a few moments' work that would enrich his paltry pay and enhance his standing in the eyes of his fellow officers, Eisenhower took the dare and the bet duly placed with a third party, a lieutenant named Wade "Ham" Haislip. Eisenhower discarded his uniform blouse and was partway up the cable and already counting his winnings when a gruff voice from below demanded to know who he was and what the hell he was doing hanging on to the cable. "Mr. Eisenhower, Sir," he replied at once, quickly explaining the circumstances. He begged to be allowed to complete his climb, but his irate commanding officer bellowed for Eisenhower to climb down at once. Eisenhower hastily complied and still minus his blouse, saluted his commander. Eisenhower never forgot his first severe chewing out as a U.S. Army officer, as Colonel Waltz enlightened his new lieutenant about his many shortcomings. "Foolhardy," "undignified," "untrustworthy," "undependable," and "ignorant" were among the attributes mentioned.

Eisenhower, however, seemed more concerned about losing his precious five-dollar bet than with the fact that he had just made an appalling first impression on his commanding officer. A loud quarrel ensued when he refused to pay off, arguing that he would easily have won had the colonel not interfered. Tempers flared as the two officers argued, with Eisenhower offering to settle the matter of who won with his fists. Reason prevailed, and the bet was declared a draw. Eisenhower's knee was again bothering him, and he later admitted relief that he had not had to fight a much larger opponent and possibly further injure himself.[13]

Throughout his military career, the one army custom Eisenhower despised above all others was the courtesy call. A newly arrived officer was expected to visit the quarters of his superiors and formally introduce himself. It was acceptable to leave one's calling card at the residence in lieu of the visit if the officer was not at home. Eisenhower thought the practice tedious and, never comfortable engaging in small talk with people for whom he cared not a whit, would deliberately wait until the regimental officers were attending a function to leave his card. As John remembers, "This was a chore that Dad detested and he made little secret of it."[14]

Like any other inexperienced new officer, Eisenhower had a great deal to learn. To absorb and master the duties of a junior officer was one thing, but the most important and clearly the most difficult aspect of his new profession was to earn the respect of his men. Eisenhower set about the task with a determination to perform well without drawing undue attention to himself.

When it came to army politics, he rapidly absorbed the rules of the game and executed them to near perfection. Even though he was known for occasional instances of compassion and forgiveness of military transgressions (for example, condoning the unauthorized wearing of his dress shoes by his enlisted orderly), during the first years of his career, Eisenhower was a stern disciplinarian who once punished an errant soldier by ordering him to dig a very large, very deep hole and then to fill it in.

In a profession in which discipline was the cornerstone of daily life, Eisenhower was soon well regarded by his men and his superiors, a laudable achievement for a young officer. Early in his career Eisenhower also demonstrated a special interest in the welfare of his troops, especially the food they ate. One of the additional duties routinely assigned new second lieutenants is that of mess officer, which, for most, is a most unwelcome task. Eisenhower, however, was delighted. The experience gained during his youth in Abilene merely enhanced his love of food and cooking. He attended a course on cooking and managing mess-hall operations. From that time forth, the proper feeding of troops became an important focus, and those who failed to measure up to his standards earned his wrath. From 1915 through his tenure as army chief of staff after World War II, Eisenhower never forgot the maxim that an army travels on its stomach, and woe to the officer who took his mess duties lightly. "I have made things miserable on occasion," he remarked, "for young captains or lieutenants, responsible for messes, who limited their inspection to questioning whether pots and pans were shined brightly enough."[15]

It was at this time, too, that Bob Davis's lessons in the art of poker began to pay off handsomely for a young man of limited means. Eisenhower had no trouble finding eager poker-playing benefactors who generally lost to him. Once he reluctantly joined a game with only two silver dollars in his pocket. He won one hundred dollars and as he began cashing out to keep a date with his new girlfriend, the two big losers demanded that he stay and give them a chance to win their money back. Eisenhower refused and instead offered to bet each fifty dollars that they could not win a single roll of the dice. They declined to call his bluff. Although Eisenhower used his bountiful profit and his back pay from June to reimburse the Leavenworth tailor for his uniforms, he had yet to repay his father's loan.

With so little for the army to do in peacetime, sports, particularly football, rated very high on most commanders' list of priorities. Good coaches were hard to find, and Eisenhower's experience coaching football at West Point was an entry on his résumé that he came to regret shortly after arriving at Fort Sam Houston. Although he loved coaching, he abhorred being assigned to a post solely because he was wanted as the football coach. Eisenhower correctly concluded that having a primary attribute "coach" affixed to his name was hardly a route to higher promotions and top-level assignments.

Yet, he was frequently to become the target of zealous commanders who saw Eisenhower not as competent career-officer material but as a present-day successful football coach. It did not help that being so junior, he was at the mercy of the whims of his superiors.

In the autumn of 1915, Eisenhower was approached by the superintendent of the Peacock Military Academy, a local private school, and asked if he would coach its football team. For his services he would be paid $150, a handsome stipend for one still deeply in debt. Although tempted, Eisenhower decided that coaching was incompatible with his duties and rejected the offer.

General officers are rarely in the habit of seeking out a junior officer to ask for a favor, and even less inclined to buy them drinks at the officers' club. However, not long afterward, Maj. Gen. Frederick Funston, the commanding general of the Southern Department (also located at Fort Sam), appeared there without warning and asked, "Is Mr. Eisenhower in the room?" Eisenhower and several friends were drinking beer, and he immediately stood up and replied, "Sir?" wondering why he had been sought out. The general ordered drinks, then got to the point. The superintendent had been in touch with him about Eisenhower. "It would please me and it would be good for the Army if you would accept this offer," Funston said. Although tactfully phrased, the "request" was a none-too-subtle command for Eisenhower to change his mind. He dutifully said, "Yes, Sir," and complied. If measured solely by his success during his first coaching stint as an army officer, he would have been very highly rated indeed. The team performed well, and Eisenhower's reputation as an excellent football coach soared.

In 1916 he was again recruited, this time to coach Saint Louis College, a small Catholic parochial school in San Antonio that had not won a single football game in five years. Eisenhower's growing reputation as a successful football coach was secured when the team staged a remarkable turnaround and even reached the finals of the San Antonio city competition before losing a close championship game.

As he settled into the routine of duty with a peacetime Regular Army regiment, Eisenhower still retained powerful feelings for Gladys Harding and at first cared little about the social life of the post. One of his letters that has survived (undated, as usual) was a clear indication that he still missed her deeply and was no closer to getting over her than he had been in September.

"I just *had* to write," he penned to Gladys. "Made me feel sad and lonesome. Somehow when I get into a rather rebellious mood, I can't enjoy life at all. I was so happy last summer. And now—seems that you are sort of 'drifting'—as you said you would. . . . With me its [*sic*] the same routine day after day, and I have all my evenings to just *think* of you. I live in memories and in hopes. You are so desirable and lovely—and honey, how I miss you . . . write me a letter and make it *big*—tell me all I *want* to hear . . . girl—you are concerned in everything I do—or think—why you are *all* to me." Under his signature Eisenhower wrote: "I've done been true, my gal, to you."[16]

He did not remain so for long. Eisenhower's first stint as officer of the day on a Sunday in October 1915 changed his life forever. The Fort Sam Houston BOQ were situated along Infantry Row and across the street from the officers' club. On either side were the quarters of married officers. As Eisenhower emerged from his quarters smartly attired, with a pistol strapped to his waist and wearing a campaign hat cocked at a jaunty angle in imitation of those worn by Teddy Roosevelt's Rough Riders, he was hailed by Lulu Ingrum Harris, the wife of Maj. Hunter Harris, an officer assigned to Eisenhower's regiment. A group was lounging on the steps and lawn of the Harrises' quarters enjoying the late-afternoon sunshine, sipping grape juice, and gossiping. Lulu Harris called out, "Come here, Ike. I want to introduce you to some friends."

Her friends consisted of two bachelor officers and a group of civilians, among them several young women. One of the officers was Lt. Leonard T. "Gee" Gerow, a graduate of the Virginia Military Institute, with whom Eisenhower began a lifelong friendship that would take them from the halls of military academe at Fort Leavenworth to the Normandy beachhead and the Battle of the Bulge.

Eisenhower brushed off Lulu Harris by replying that he was on duty and could not spare the time. Then he noticed that one of the group was a very attractive young woman dressed in a white summer frock, and promptly changed his mind. He was introduced to John and Elvira Mathilde Carlson Doud and their three daughters. The Douds were a well-to-do Denver family who wintered each year in an upscale section of San Antonio. John Sheldon Doud, a businessman of English descent, was a doting father to his pampered daughters and was called "Pupah" by his family. His wife, Elvira, who was called Nana by her family, was a child of first-generation Swedish parents.[17]

John Doud was a restless and adventuresome fellow who, by the age of eighteen, had already run away from home three times. When he eventually settled down, Doud rose from rags to riches managing the family meatpacking business in Boone, Iowa, becoming a millionaire at a very young age. When Nana's health began to suffer in the harsh climate of Iowa, John Doud relocated his family to the friendlier climate of Colorado, settling first in Colorado Springs, and later moving to an exclusive Denver neighborhood in deference to their eldest daughter, Eleanor. She was born exceptionally frail, and by an early age had developed a serious heart condition that was exacerbated by the high altitude of Colorado Springs. Her decline was steady, and she died in 1912, aged seventeen, causing untold grief in the Doud family.[18]

John Doud had few intimate friends, was secretive about his private life, and is said to have kept two mistresses under assumed names he created to deceive the two women and his wife. He endured a lifetime of disappointment that Nana was unable to present him with a male heir. As partial compensation, two of his other daughters were given male nicknames. Still, he lavished all the trappings of the good life on his daughters. Papa Doud was especially close to his second child, Mamie Geneva Doud, who was born in Boone on November 14, 1896. He lovingly called Mamie "Little Puddy"; she called him "Pooh-Bah." Of the three surviving Doud girls, Mamie had, by 1915, become the most proficient at inducing him to cater to her every whim.

In San Antonio it was customary for the family to take a Sunday-afternoon drive in John Doud's electric car. By happenstance the Douds were present at the Harris quarters when Lt. Dwight Eisenhower appeared and was introduced to Miss Mamie Geneva Doud. A spirited eighteen-year-old socialite who had recently completed Miss Wolcott's (Finishing) School in Denver, Mamie later admitted to an instant attraction to the twenty-five-year-old officer, whom she thought was "the handsomest man" she had ever met.

Eisenhower thought her vivacious and saucy, with an intriguing air of impertinence. The flirtatious Mamie Doud tried but seems to have failed to disguise her reciprocal interest in Eisenhower, despite a warning from Lulu Harris that he was well known as Fort Sam's "woman-hater."[19] For Mamie the comment was as if Lulu had waved the proverbial red flag. She would later say of the man who became her husband, "Ike has the most engaging grin of anybody I ever met. Though when he turns it off his face is as bleak as the plains of Kansas."[20]

Within moments of their first meeting, Eisenhower impulsively asked Miss Doud if she would care to accompany him as he inspected the guard posts. Eisenhower's invitation was as unconventional as it was daring for an unattached female civilian—even one as fascinating as Mamie Doud—to accompany an officer making his official rounds. To his surprise Mamie accepted, "though I loathed walking." As they passed the troop barracks during their stroll, Eisenhower formally explained that she might see or hear things unsuitable for a young lady and urged her to keep her eyes straight ahead. Mamie, of course, did the exact opposite. Nevertheless their lengthy promenade around the post was agonizing for Mamie, who was wearing fashionable new shoes that were wholly inappropriate for walking. "I never walked so far in my life," she remembered. Eisenhower then asked Mamie for a date. Shocked, she refused, pointing out that her social calendar was already booked for some weeks ahead.

Although described as "an outrageous flirt" in her debutante year, Mamie Doud had actually dated relatively few young men. Her social status notwithstanding, Mamie was then unworldly and, by her own admission, naive.

Compared to the "lounge lizards with patent-leather hair," as she referred to the sons of the Denver social crowd, Mamie found the smooth-talking Eisenhower an alluring combination of brashness and manliness.

The following day Eisenhower telephoned the Doud home only to learn that Mamie had gone fishing with another beau. From then on he would call two or three times daily, only to be informed by the maid that Mamie was not available or by Mamie herself that her datebook was full for the next three weeks. "What did he expect? I was booked solid. It was my debutante year!"[21] When that ploy failed to sway Mamie into reserving a date for him, Eisenhower began showing up unannounced and uninvited at the Doud home. Mamie was frequently out on a date, and he would patiently sit on the porch awaiting her return. He used the time to good advantage by doing his best to impress her parents. Eisenhower's relentless pursuit of Mamie was part of a deliberate plan to make himself her only suitor by discouraging his would-be rivals, who would note his frequent presence at the Doud home as evidence that he had cornered her affections.

Still, for a time the romance went nowhere. Although Mamie had had little experience with men, she had mastered the skill of intentionally stimulating Eisenhower's growing interest by playing hard to get. After several weeks of this game, John Doud scolded Mamie "to stop her flighty nonsense or the 'Army boy' will give up in disgust."[22]

Mamie took the hint, and after a month of amorous denial, the spoiled Denver socialite and the acknowledged "woman-hater" of Fort Sam Houston began an improbable courtship. From then on Eisenhower became a fixture at the Doud household, and before long the two were dating each other exclusively. They went to places Eisenhower could barely afford: a vaudeville show, an occasional dance on the roof of a downtown hotel, and numerous meals at an inexpensive Mexican restaurant.[23] Unable to support himself, court Mamie, and pay off his debts, Eisenhower was usually broke before the end of the month, and lived from hand to mouth until the next payday. Nevertheless at Christmas 1915, possibly paying with poker winnings, Eisenhower managed to present Mamie with an expensive, engraved jewelry box. Even though such a gift violated Doud protocol, Mamie swayed her parents into letting her keep it.

Eisenhower's charm handily won over the Douds, with the lone exception of Mamie's spiteful eight-year-old sister Mabel Frances ("Mike"), who perceived him as a serious threat to the family's equilibrium and did everything in her power to make his visits miserable. "When her parents weren't looking," wrote one of Mamie's biographers, "she bit, kicked and scratched her big sister's caller. Mamie and Ike gave her as wide a berth as possible, but 'Mike,' even in her less violent moods, would thunder up and down the north porch, screeching insults."[24]

For Dwight Eisenhower, raised in the Spartan atmosphere of a home where he never observed his parents embrace each other or exchange a harsh word, life with the Douds was an eye-opening introduction to an utterly different form of family life. Sentimental and demonstrative, they spoke their minds, argued frequently, threw tantrums, cried, and made up. Where John Doud was outgoing and doted on his family, the dour David Eisenhower apparently endured a life of utter joylessness.

John Doud's grandson and namesake, John Sheldon Doud Eisenhower, who spent considerable time with the Douds as a young man, found the family passionate but excessive in their frequent displays of emotion with one another. "I came from the kind of family," said Mamie, "where if one of us was going around the corner we all kissed her goodbye and then went to the window to wave her out of sight."[25]

John Eisenhower thought John Doud "regarded Ike as a son" he never had, and "Nana just doted on him."[26] As time passed it was strikingly evident that Eisenhower greatly preferred the company of the Douds to that of his own family. Nana was captivated by Eisenhower and, "after we were married," remembered Mamie, "I learned quickly not to run to her seeking comfort when my husband and I had a spat. She always sided with Ike. The two had a great liking and respect for each other."[27]

By early 1916 Eisenhower had won over Mamie, yet remained as restless as ever, writing to Ruby Norman: "My life here is, in the main, uninteresting—nothing much doing—and I get tired of the same old grind some times. The girl I'm running around with now is named Miss Doud, from Denver. Winters here. Pretty nice—but awful strong for society—which often bores me. But we get on well together—and I'm at her house whenever I'm off duty." Eisenhower's heartache over Gladys Harding's rejection of his marriage proposal obviously still rankled. Although pleased when Gladys sent him an expensive smoking jacket for Christmas, he concluded his letter to Ruby Norman by remarking, "Sometime, if you are interested, I'll tell you all about the girl I run around with *since* I learned that G. H. cared so terribly for her work."[28]

Unlike his proposal of marriage to Gladys Harding, Eisenhower never formally asked Mamie to marry him. As their courtship deepened both simply *assumed* they would one day marry. On Valentine's Day in 1916, Eisenhower presented Mamie with a miniature replica of his class ring—the traditional custom when a West Pointer becomes engaged. Mamie would have none of it, insisting that she wanted and would accept nothing less than a *full-size* ring. She got one and proudly wore it throughout their marriage. The couple decided to wed in November 1916, on Mamie's twentieth birthday.

Still apprehensive about his continual lack of funds and all too aware that he would have to find some means of properly supporting Mamie when they married, Eisenhower applied for aviation duty with the forerunner of what would become the Army Air Service. Army aviation was then under the aegis of the Signal Corps, and his acceptance would mean a not-inconsequential 50 percent increase in pay. Moreover, flying fascinated him, and the attraction of becoming one of the army's elite pioneer aviators was irresistible. "I'll get a lot more then," he told Ruby Norman, "and maybe I can make ends meet. Ha Ha—you know me—I'll never have a sou."[29]

Though troubled by the notion of her fiancé entering an untested, dangerous vocation, Mamie was surprisingly supportive when Eisenhower was quickly accepted. Eisenhower remembered how he had eagerly anticipated the experience. Mr. Doud had graciously given his permission for their union, even though he and Nana both thought Mamie far too young to be married at age twenty. When Eisenhower arrived at the Doud home he remembers "walking on air" until he told the assembled Douds that he would soon become an aviator. Eisenhower's announcement was greeted with chilling silence and stony disapproval from John Doud.

Aviation was then in its infancy, untested and unsafe. The first active aviation unit operated in Mexico in short-lived support of the so-called punitive expedition. The inexperienced First Aero Squadron was equipped with the dangerously unstable Curtiss JN-2 "Jennies." The gallant men who flew these death traps were all pioneer aviators. Three of them—Carl Spaatz, Millard Harmon, and Ralph Royce—would become prominent commanders in the Army Air Corps during World War II. A number of other young lieutenants and captains assigned to the punitive expedition were also destined for high rank, and for a close future association with Dwight Eisenhower: George S. Patton, Courtney H. Hodges, William H. Simpson, Kenyon A. Joyce (a future commanding officer of both Eisenhower and Patton), Lesley J. McNair, and Brehon B. Somervell.[30]

The six Jennies lasted barely one month before all crashed. Two were lost within the first week of the expedition. Despite their brief participation in the punitive expedition to carry mail and dispatches, the need for aviation in a modern war was affirmed.[31]

His courtship of Mamie Doud had not quenched Eisenhower's thirst for action. Pershing's punitive expedition was the perfect chance, but his request for a transfer was rejected. Despite his obvious affection for Eisenhower, John Doud was deeply troubled at the prospect of his beloved daughter marrying someone about to become part of an untested and inherently hazardous profession. He balked at subjecting his Mamie to such perils, and threatened to withdraw his approval if Eisenhower carried out his irresponsible intention. It was bad enough that Mamie would live under greatly reduced economic and social circumstances, but the notion of her also becoming a widow was too much. Mamie argued in vain with her father that Eisenhower should be permitted to follow his dream. Faced with accepting the aviation assignment or very possibly losing Mamie, Eisenhower hesitated for several days before relenting and announcing to the assembled Douds that he would pass up becoming an aviator. Notwithstanding his later claim to have had no regrets about his decision, Eisenhower never lost his enthusiasm for flying or his desire to qualify as a pilot.

That Eisenhower fell for and married Mamie Doud on the rebound from the unhappy end of his romance with Gladys Harding is unequivocal. Moreover, it is likely that sometime in early 1916 Gladys sent Eisenhower a "Dear John" letter, most likely after she learned of Eisenhower's intention to marry Mamie, when she knew for certain they would have no future together.

Whether out of love or need, Gladys Harding left the music circuit for good in 1916 and returned to Abilene. She later revealed to Ruby Norman's daughter that she had expected to marry Eisenhower and that the news of his engagement to Mamie Doud was crushing. "Gladys *had* to be married before Eisenhower, and she was, sixteen days before"—in June 1916, to an older local man named Cecil Brooks, a widower whose first wife had died the previous year during childbirth. Brooks's previous overtures toward Gladys had been rebuffed until she learned that Dwight Eisenhower was marrying another. In short order she married Cecil Brooks, a man she barely knew, solely "to spite Dwight." Indeed, her impulsive and emotional decision doomed Eisenhower's first love to a joyless marriage that lasted until Cecil Brooks's death in 1944. Afterward, Gladys suffered a nervous breakdown from what Ruby Norman was convinced was overwhelming guilt at never having loved Cecil Brooks.[32]

In the years before it was recognized as a deadly health menace, smoking was considered fashionable. Eisenhower's smoking habit, begun at West Point, continued unabated despite his forthcoming marriage to Mamie. As a concession to his more serious new attitude, Eisenhower proudly but foolishly stopped smoking ready-made cigarettes and reverted to the roll-your-own variety to save money. Eisenhower smoked heavily until 1949, when he was sternly warned by his doctor to stop or face serious consequences. He did so cold turkey, and, although he never again touched a cigarette, it has since become clear that nearly forty years of smoking that ranged from moderate to uncurbed excess eventually took its toll on Eisenhower's already questionable health.[33] Mamie also smoked for many years, probably beginning about the time she met Ike. Whether or not he influenced her decision to start is not known but she was never a heavy smoker like her husband and eventually stopped in her later years.[34]

The Douds returned to Denver soon after the engagement was announced, and the courtship continued by letter. Initially their plans did not take into account the expanding global war in Europe and the beginning of mass mobilization in the United States. Mamie was hardly reassured by the knowledge that her fiancé was intent on sticking his neck out, if not in aviation, then either in Mexico or Europe. Frightened that "[she] might lose him," she privately vowed to marry Ike as soon as possible, regardless of the anticipated objections from her parents.

The initiative actually came from Eisenhower, who telephoned in late June and said, "Let's get married *now.*" Mamie still had to overcome the small matter of notifying and obtaining permission from her parents, who were away on a trip to Iowa. They were "speechless" at the news and "raised the roof," recalled Mamie. "They had the old-fashioned notion that quick weddings weren't quite decent." Mamie Doud had to employ all her powers of persuasion to overcome the Douds' serious misgivings that such a brief engagement might wrongly convey an impression that the marriage was a matter of urgency rather than of choice. "But I was stubborn. Finally, Mama gave in and pretty soon she brought Papa around."[35]

Their timing could not have been much worse. The army was on a virtual war footing, and ordinary furloughs were cancelled for the duration. Eisenhower requested a twenty-day leave to marry Mamie and was bewildered when he was summoned to appear before General Funston to explain himself. Such is the discretion of general officers that—although in direct violation of War Department policy—Funston nevertheless granted Lieutenant Eisenhower a ten-day leave. Undoubtedly Funston's generosity was a subtle reward to Eisenhower for having coached football the year before.

With the wedding only a short time off, Eisenhower was again broke and in dire need of a wedding ring for Mamie, as well as funds for travel and a brief honeymoon. He persuaded a jeweler to sell him a ring on credit, and a local bank agreed to cover the overdrafts he expected to incur.

The first two and a half days of his furlough consisted of a frustrating, flood-delayed journey by train from San Antonio to Denver. Eisenhower's marriage to Mamie Geneva Doud was a family-only ceremony performed in the music room of the Doud home at noon on July 1, 1916, the same day the army promoted him to the rank of first lieutenant. In a scene reminiscent of the summer of 1913 in Abilene, Eisenhower stood virtually motionless for two hours before the ceremony to avoid creasing his immaculate white dress uniform. The short notice meant that the family pastor was not available, and the wedding ceremony was instead conducted by an English clergyman whom the family barely knew. The honeymoon was necessarily short, at a nearby resort hotel to which the couple traveled by train.

No correspondence has survived, and his memoir is unhelpful in answering the question of just when Eisenhower notified his parents of his engagement and forthcoming marriage. Their return to San Antonio was via Abilene, to meet his family, and then Kansas City, where they would visit his brother Arthur. The tiresome train journey from Denver to Abilene was hot and uncomfortable, and when they arrived in Abilene about 3:00 A.M., Mamie discovered that, in a parting prank, her two younger sisters had filled her powder box with rice. They were met by David, whom she found polite and rather shy. Mamie's first impression was that Mr. Eisenhower had defied the accepted social custom of her world by not wearing a coat when outside.

Mamie quickly discerned that the Eisenhowers were unlike any family she had ever encountered, and that she had no more in common with the senior Eisenhowers than she did with her bridegroom. She was appalled at the amount of work Ida performed and surprised at the family's lack of worldliness. They neither drank, smoked, nor played cards and appeared not to enjoy life as she knew it. During later visits to Abilene, in deference to her in-laws Mamie would smoke furtively, leaning out of an upstairs window, "hoping she wouldn't be caught."[36]

While she found Ida friendly and outgoing, Mamie never warmed to David, even though she politely addressed them as "Grandma" and "Grandpa." "Ike's father was a good man but to me he always seemed stern. . . . The boys owed everything to their mother." Nor was she ever truly at ease in the Eisenhower home during their infrequent visits to Abilene, particularly in summertime when the brass bedsteads were too hot to touch. "I got out of there in a hurry, I'll tell you, every time I got the chance."

Mamie also became an unwitting participant in the continuing fantasy surrounding David Eisenhower, once relating Milton Good's alleged treachery to an interviewer, concluding, "He [David] had taken engineering by mail, so he went to Texas and took a job as [a] construction engineer."[37]

Not surprisingly Eisenhower seemed increasingly uncomfortable around his parents but completely at ease with the Douds, whose company he far preferred.[38] John Eisenhower's observation is instructive: "The Eisenhowers were so rigidly Pennsylvania Dutch, I don't think Dad communicated on a confidential basis with his father, *ever*."[39]

However, when Mamie met Milton for the first time, she planted a kiss on his cheek and said how much she had always wanted to have a brother. Milton was captivated. "And I've been her willing slave ever since!"[40] Mamie adored Milton, and over the years he became a treasured part of her inner circle of close friends.

Ida had prepared an enormous feast to welcome them. Although the visit lasted a mere eight hours, its impression on Mamie was indelible. The newlyweds departed for Kansas City with their bellies stuffed with Ida's finest cooking. After a reunion with Arthur they entrained for San Antonio to begin married life, arriving just as Eisenhower's leave expired. Their journey to San Antonio was on the Katy railroad, which passed through Denison, Texas, and within a few yards of his birthplace.[41]

Part III
WORLD WAR I, 1917–1919

Woe to him who sets Europe ablaze.

—FIELD MARSHAL HELMUTH VON MOLTKE

10.

Roses Have Thorns

Mamie, there is one thing you must understand.
My country comes first and always will; you come second.

First Lieutenant and Mrs. Dwight Eisenhower returned to Fort Sam Houston and the congratulations of friends and colleagues, who showered the couple with badly needed presents. They moved into Eisenhower's two-room apartment in the BOQ along Infantry Row. Marriage would toughen Mamie to a world she had no conception even existed: one in which there were no servants and the comforts of an upper-class home were replaced by drab, Lilliputian military quarters designed for spartan utility. She rented a piano for five dollars per month, and Ike installed a wooden icebox in their bathroom. However, Mamie frequently neglected to empty the drainage pan, resulting in a flood in their parlor.

Many years later Mamie candidly admitted that they had had little in common when they married. Indeed, Mamie Geneva Doud and Dwight David Eisenhower were a classic romantic mismatch, with almost nothing in common but love. Their granddaughter, Susan, has aptly described their union as "an attraction of opposites" in which each took the best qualities from the other. One was born into a family of high social status and wanted for nothing, yet was utterly unsophisticated about the world outside her immediate social circle; the other was the product of an impoverished childhood, who was cocksure but uncomfortable in the presence of women.

Mamie had never cooked a meal, happily endorsing her mother's dictum that: "If you don't learn to cook, no one will ask you to do it."[1] Never having been obliged to so much as make her own bed, the overindulged Mamie regarded housekeeping as a duty to be performed by servants. In a reversal of roles, Eisenhower was an expert at cooking and was no stranger to every conceivable household chore. For a time the couple ate all their meals at the officers' club, but the expense eventually grew too great on a salary that inevitably ran out before month's end. Fortunately her husband's love of cooking saved the newlyweds from a daily gastronomical fiasco. Finally "she allowed

Ike to teach her some basic cooking skills, and they started to eat simply at home."[2]

No matter how inadequate or uncomfortable their apartment was, Mamie kept an immaculate house, entertained in accordance with military custom, and helped turn the Eisenhower quarters at Fort Sam (and later at other duty stations), into a social refuge for Ike's military friends, who always received a warm welcome at what was eventually christened "Club Eisenhower."[3] "Ike is the kind," said Mamie, "who would rather give you a fried egg in his own home than take you to the finest night club in the world." They had no radio, and evenings were often spent reading. Eisenhower remained an inveterate reader, continuing to expand his knowledge of military history. "In our home everyone does as he pleases. If Ike wants to read, he reads or takes a nap." In addition to practicing his cooking skills, what pleased him most was good conversation. Mamie judged him a fascinating talker: "At any party there is always a group around Ike." His thirst for information had turned him into a very good listener. "If you were interviewing him, you would find yourself doing all the talking."[4]

She had also entered the provincial world of the Regular Army, which itself was a rude awakening. For the first time Mamie was exposed to the camaraderie of other women, with whom she stoically endured the hardships of frequent moves, miserable quarters, the long hours her husband worked, and a meager income. The most unrewarding aspect of military life, however was the gossip, the pettiness, and backstabbing of some military wives—bored or ambitious women who advanced their own agendas, ranging from promoting their husbands' careers to avenging real or imagined slights. Mamie would have none of it and refused to play this game or to engage in such trivia, which she disavowed.

On the positive side, military families tended to look out for one another. Mamie found other wives who were friendly and supportive. It was customary to welcome new arrivals with a helping hand in the form of food or the loan of household items until the family could settle in. "We all did it, everybody helped out," remembered Mamie. Other young couples became part of the Eisenhowers' social circle, all of them sharing a common bond of being at the bottom of the army's social and military pecking order. Before long Mamie had become very popular with the other wives for her friendliness and endearing manner, traits that were perhaps her strongest contributions to her new husband's budding career.

In addition, Mamie's friends in the San Antonio community provided a welcome outlet from the Fort Sam social routine. Their social life included frequent trips to town to eat or go dancing, as they had during their brief courtship. The arrival of her family for their annual sojourn in San Antonio was also a great source of comfort. When Nana visited in the autumn of 1916, the change in her daughter was noticeable: "Four months of married responsibility had tamed her social butterfly to a serious housewife, one who was perhaps too worried about household matters."[5]

Mamie viewed her role as strictly that of a homemaker whose function was to focus on making her husband content by creating a tranquil home environment. For all her inexperience, she strove mightily to become a good army wife, once saying, "You can't be much help to your husband but you can do a lot to hurt him."[6] Fifty-six years later, as Mamie looked back on her marriage to Eisenhower, she expressed her gratitude. "I'd say to God every day, 'I'm so thankful.' . . . I don't know exactly how to explain it, but everything was a pattern, like it had been planned. But it wasn't planned by us. God planned it."[7]

Unlike his verbal outpouring of love for Gladys Harding, Eisenhower was rarely able to express his love for Mamie. Julie Nixon Eisenhower once remarked that whereas Mamie's emotions were an open book—"every complaint, every thought, petty or important"—Eisenhower "to his dying day, found it difficult to express his feelings." Even on the joyous occasion of the birth of their first child, Eisenhower's love for his wife and newborn son was kept safely locked within.[8]

Mamie thought Ike worked too hard but kept her opinion to herself with the observation that, "No woman can run him."[9] Nothing, however, could have adequately prepared her for a role as the wife of a poorly paid army officer in a profession that was, at best, regarded with indifference in the world outside the military. From the outset she made it a point never to involve herself in her husband's business. His work problems remained in the office, not in the Eisenhower household. During their fifty-two years of marriage, Mamie Eisenhower never wavered in her dedication to her husband and his career. In later years stories about Mamie would trumpet such headlines as HER CAREER IS IKE. In today's more liberated age, Mamie Eisenhower might inaccurately be portrayed as a classic example of a (military) wife in a Victorian age of male chauvinism where the husband was the boss; where *his* views were regarded as gospel; where wives were seen but not heard; and where their role was to cook, raise the kids, and provide a happy and contented home.

Much like her mother-in-law, Mamie exercised her own form of influence. In public she never expressed opinions or openly disagreed with Ike. Unlike the fiery Beatrice Patton, who once swung a sword at her husband's head when he took her for granted, and physically attacked a portly, deskbound Washington colonel who insulted her husband, Mamie was undemonstrative in public. She once told her granddaughter-in-law, Julie Nixon Eisenhower, "There can be only one star in the heaven, Sugar, and there is only one way to live with an Eisenhower. Let him have his own way."[10]

One of Eisenhower's presidential speechwriters once opined, "Ike would have been *Colonel* Dwight D. Eisenhower, if it weren't for Mamie."[11] Over time Mamie's influence would grow, and she would later avow, "Ike took care of the office—I ran the house." This included the family finances, which she ran thriftily and efficiently, thanks to her mother, who had trained Mamie how to budget the family finances, keep meticulous records, and economize.

Perhaps it was a lucky omen that Eisenhower was promoted to first lieutenant on his wedding day, thenceforth to earn a princely extra twenty dollars per month. John Doud announced that he would not subsidize their income; the couple would have to learn to subsist on Ike's pay. He did, however, present them with a four-year-old Pullman automobile and a cash gift, part of which was spent to furnish their quarters. The remainder was jealously hoarded by Mamie in her role of family banker. Although thereafter the Eisenhowers were never without an automobile, courtesy of Pupah, despite Mamie's valiant efforts to "squeeze a dollar until the eagle screamed" by making Ike's pay last through the entire month, it was often a losing battle. "Many a time we were down to our last twenty-five cents when payday dawned."[12] Mamie would later proudly state: "There may have been times when we had only a dollar in the bank, but we have never owed a cent in our lives."[13]

John Doud never fully carried out his plan not to support his daughter and son-in-law, and after the birth of their first child in 1917, he sent Mamie one hundred dollars monthly. During the trying interwar years and the Great Depression, it was this monthly stipend that enabled Eisenhower to remain in the army at a time when he seriously considered resigning for a better-paying civilian job.[14]

If there were already definite signs of change and a growing maturity as a result of his marriage, there would soon be emerging evidence that behaviorally Eisenhower was a classic type A personality. "Such an individual," notes Eisenhower scholar Robert Ferrell, "is careless about health, immoderate in regard to working hours, driven by the need to go at top speed day after day." Brig. Gen. Thomas Mattingly, one of Eisenhower's presidential physicians, thoroughly investigated his entire history of health problems and concluded, "As a youth Eisenhower showed none of the driving ambition and the tension that later became so obvious. Perhaps it was there but no one recorded it." Yet, as Ferrell notes, "The entire Eisenhower family had a history of hypertension, cardiovascular disease . . . and coronary disease."[15]

Between their money woes and Eisenhower's poor health, the marriage was far from easy. In December 1916 he contracted malaria and was confined to his quarters for eight days. Several months later, in March 1917, tonsillitis resulted in another six days at home. In May, the malaria recurred, and Eisenhower was sent home for ten more days until the fever passed.[16] Although the malaria would not return, Eisenhower's military career would be marked by a variety of health problems.

One of Eisenhower's assigned duties was that of provost marshal, the military version of a chief of police. It was a position that kept Eisenhower and the military police hopping. Numerous brawls in San Antonio, usually alcohol related, broke out between national guardsmen and Regular Army soldiers. To help prevent incidents Eisenhower and several MPs would visit the local bars and brothels and arrest those who were being unruly or were found to be AWOL. One night a drunken national guard lieutenant fired two pistol rounds at Eisenhower from a nearby alley, nearly killing him. The incident shook Eisenhower so badly he feared for Mamie's safety on a military post where there were few women. He presented Mamie with a .45 pistol and taught her its proper use in an emergency. However, when he attempted to test her reaction to a simulated break-in, Eisenhower discovered that she had hidden it so well that "she couldn't have gotten it out in a week, much less in a hurry. I decided to concentrate on making the camp safer."[17]

The Douds had always been very formal, and the girls were required to present themselves in proper dress for meals, even breakfast. Mamie's modest economic means notwithstanding, throughout her marriage she always worked strenuously to maintain herself as glamorously as possible for her husband. On the dubious recommendation of her doctor, who claimed it would do wonders for the skin of her face, she often spent one day a week in bed. He seems to have noticed and appreciated Mamie's appearance and fastidious dress. From the time he met Mamie, Eisenhower would become annoyed whenever he encountered women who were improperly or sloppily dressed in public.[18]

Ike's West Point classmates were surprised at his marriage. Although it was customary for an officer who married to notify the academy jeweler, who would then send him a gift from the class, which each officer would help pay for, Eisenhower had not bothered. Thus, when Lt. (later Maj. Gen.) John B. Wogan was passing through San Antonio and decided to visit Eisenhower, "The door was opened by a pretty girl wearing an apron and holding a broom . . . we'd always considered him the true bachelor type—a good bet for the last man in the class to get married. Who was this girl?

"I stood at the open door, embarrassed, and inquired in my best stammer if she knew the whereabouts of Lieutenant Eisenhower. She replied that he was drilling with his company; would I like to come in and wait for him? . . . My confusion obviously amused her. Finally, she rescued me. 'I'm Mrs. Eisenhower,' she said smiling. 'Ike and I were married on the first of July.' "[19]

The instability that had racked Mexico since 1910 had, by 1914, evolved into increasing hostility to the United States, principally over Woodrow

Wilson's interference in Mexican affairs and his inept handling of U.S.-Mexican relations. After longtime dictator Porfirio Díaz was overthrown in 1910, there followed a period of revolution and turmoil in which a short-lived democratic government was itself overthrown by a military coup in 1913. Wilson refused to recognize the new regime, and an incident in Tampico and the occupation of Veracruz in 1914 by an American military force was an attempt by the president to persuade the Mexican people to replace yet another in a long line of despots. The ploy backfired, instead exacerbating the growing anti-Americanism in Mexico. The United States withheld recognition and sent military supplies to the regime's opponent, Venustiano Carranza, a former senator, wealthy landowner, and a ruthless revolutionary.

Among Carranza's early supporters was a charismatic renegade from Durango named Francisco Villa, who was better known to his legion of followers as "Pancho." A notorious bandit leader and folk hero, Villa epitomized the Mexicans' love of *macho* and had become the Latino version of Robin Hood, looting the rich, rustling their cattle, and giving to the poor. Villa's folk-hero stature notwithstanding, he was also a cold-blooded killer who "could shoot down a man point-blank, showing no more emotion than if he were stepping on a bug."[20]

The Veracruz incident brought about the installation of Carranza as president. The ambitious Villa broke with Carranza and began opposing his former cohort. The Mexican economy was in disarray, and instability grew as intrigue and lawlessness swept the nation. Villa had counted on American support to obtain the presidency. Instead, when Wilson recognized the new Carranza government in October 1915, an irate Villa swore revenge on the United States.[21]

By the end of 1915 not only had Villa and his *pistoleros* launched a series of raids along the U.S.-Mexican border, but Carranza's forces were engaged in similar burning and looting. Mexico was swept by violence as Villistas, Carranzistas, and several other factions reduced the nation to a state of virtual anarchy. Wilson, who had once supported Villa, now regarded him as little more than a bandit who threatened the security of the southwestern United States. Fighting appeared imminent as the War Department began deploying troops to Texas and New Mexico.

True to his threat, in early January 1916, Villa began a bloody campaign against the United States. The kidnapping and execution of sixteen American mining engineers left the United States on a virtual war footing. Early on March 9, 1916, Villa and his army of between four and five hundred men raided the small border town of Columbus, New Mexico, and began indiscriminate burning, looting, and killing. The Columbus raid left eighteen Americans dead, and although Mexican losses were very high, Villa had achieved his aim of arousing the United States.[22] A punitive expedition was quickly formed under the command of Brig. Gen. John J. "Black Jack" Pershing, a harsh disciplinarian who was considered the army's premier soldier.

The news excited Eisenhower, who immediately applied for a transfer to the punitive expedition but was summarily turned down. Nonetheless Mamie was devastated when Eisenhower returned home grim-faced one noontime in August to reveal that he had been ordered to temporary duty with the national guard. Already her first taste of army life had left her disheartened by Eisenhower's long workdays. Now, he would be away for an indeterminate time barely a month after their marriage. For an overindulged, temperamental nineteen-year-old, the prospect of her new husband's prolonged absence brought tears and complaints that fell on deaf ears. The U.S. Army, as she had quickly discovered, was a demanding and altogether formidable mistress. Mamie was "utterly accustomed to being the focus of attention," notes Susan Eisenhower, and when she "cried that Ike was leaving her, he put his arm around her and said gently, 'My duty will always come first.' Mamie understood . . . that he meant it."[23] During Eisenhower's military career there would be many more such separations, which, as she matured, Mamie learned to accept as the price of being an army wife, although she never really got over the loneliness.

Units of the national guard were mobilized for border duty, and Fort Sam Houston became the focus of the army's preparations. As one of the Regular Army officers assigned to help train the guard, Eisenhower moved to a nearby training area called Camp Wilson, where he was detailed as an inspector-instructor of the 7th Illinois ("Fighting Irish") Infantry, a unit made up almost exclusively of Chicago Irishmen. The regiment was more of a social entity than a military unit. With ill-equipped, badly trained, and decidedly unruly soldiers, scarcely a night passed when its men failed to put their motto into practice.

Eisenhower's duties included supervising close-order drill and training his charges in trench warfare, which necessitated not only digging an extensive trench system but practicing movements between positions. The regimental commander, Col. Daniel Moriarity, was a gregarious, elderly Irishman who had served under Teddy Roosevelt in the Spanish-American War. Eisenhower described him as "a fine old fellow," neglecting to mention that more often than not he was inebriated, as were numerous others (including the regimental chaplain) whose preference for drink far exceeded their interest in performing military duties. Moriarity distanced himself from training and administrative duties and virtually turned over the running of the 7th Illinois to Lieutenant Eisenhower, who was delighted to accept the de facto responsibility of running his regiment for him.

Eisenhower soon found that he not only related well to enlisted men but that his leadership was reciprocated by the high esteem in which they held him.[24] More important, the experience was an early milestone in his military career. The experience gained at Camp Wilson encouraged Eisenhower to begin taking his profession more seriously. "I began to devote more hours of study and reading to my profession," he wrote in his memoir. Yet he often did so as much from boredom as professional necessity, writing in January 1916 to Ruby Norman, "I surely hate to study. That's no fun."[25]

After one particularly ineffective trench exercise, Eisenhower bluntly asserted, "You know, colonel, if this were actual trench warfare, about half your men would be dead by now because they don't keep their heads down." Before Colonel Moriarity could reply, a quick-witted private quipped, "And you wouldn't be alive standing up there either, lieutenant." During his brief tenure with the Fighting Irish, Eisenhower developed an affinity for his charges that was fully reciprocated. By December 1916 it was abundantly clear that Pancho Villa would never be captured by the punitive expedition. The regiment was recalled from active duty and returned to Illinois, with Eisenhower present to see them off. Not only would his resourceful presence be missed, but many "felt they were losing a close friend and inspiration."[26] It was Eisenhower's first test of leadership and he had made the most of it.

As 1916 drew to a close neither Mamie nor Ike could have anticipated the stresses on their marriage that were to result from America's formal entry into World War I in April 1917. Although Ike rarely discussed his work with Mamie, he did so in December, when he broached the subject of his aspiration to transfer to the Air Corps. However, when Mamie announced she was pregnant with their first child in late December, further discussion of the Air Corps evaporated.

What had begun with a minor event in Sarajevo in June 1914—the assassination of Archduke Franz Ferdinand of Austria—had, by virtue of the complicated European linkage of treaties and alliances, escalated into a war of such dimensions that it engulfed not only Europe but the Middle East as well. By waiting until 1917, the United States avoided bloodbaths such as Gallipoli, Ypres, Arras, Passchendaele, and the Somme—horrific manifestations of the carnage that characterized World War I. On a single day—July 1, 1916—the British Army sustained 57,000 casualties, including more than 19,000 dead, in the Battle of the Somme, while at Gallipoli, British and French forces fought the Turks during an eight-month killing frenzy.[27] As appalling as these battles were, they were dwarfed by the 1916 siege of Verdun, in which the French and German armies racked up nearly 1 million casualties during the bloodiest battle in the history of warfare. By 1917 the Western Front had become a grotesque scar that ran from the North Sea across northern France to the Swiss border, and the war had evolved into a stalemate, a war of attrition in which trench warfare had become the norm in what was being called "the war to end all wars."[28]

The United States was drawn into the conflict even though Wilson and his secretary of state, William Jennings Bryan, subscribed to the belief that "a nation could remain aloof from war by refusing to prepare for it."[29] However, as relations deteriorated and Germany became more belligerent toward the United States, Wilson became more realistic about the inevitable need to employ military force. Although officially still neutral, the United States had been supporting the Allied powers—Britain, France, and Russia—with military hardware and loans that totaled nearly $1 billion, a charade that fooled no one, least of all Germany.

The Central Powers (Germany, Austria, and Turkey) were wary of the United States but undeterred from employing unlimited submarine warfare, which by early 1917 culminated in the indiscriminate sinking of Allied and neutral ships. In the end it was the aggressive acts by German U-boats that, more than anything else, goaded Wilson into seeking a declaration of war from Congress in April.[30]

War fever swiftly gripped the United States. Men rushed to volunteer in droves and posters of "Uncle Sam" appeared, proclaiming, I WANT YOU FOR U.S. ARMY. Patriotism in the form of slogans and songs swept the nation.

The decision to send an American Expeditionary Force (AEF) to France required the ablest commander in chief who could be found, an officer of proven courage and resolution to carry out the exceptionally difficult task ahead. There was only one bona fide candidate for the appointment, Black Jack Pershing, who was given a virtual carte blanche to organize the AEF. To create and train a fighting force from a tiny peacetime army, ill equipped to fight any kind of war—much less one against the formidable German army—was one of the most daunting tasks ever given to an American military commander.

The U.S. Army of 1917 was cursed with staggering shortcomings in men and equipment. The army possessed only 285,000 Springfield rifles, 544 three-inch field guns, and sufficient ammunition for a mere nine-hour bombardment. The shortage of basic weapons was so dire that the troops of one newly formed division were obliged to create mock weapons whittled from wooden sticks, a sorry state of affairs that would be replicated a quarter of a century later. Of the fifty-five planes in the fledgling Army Air Service, 93 percent were obsolete.[31]

The United States faced the daunting prospect of mobilization on a massive scale. In December 1916 the strength of the army was still a paltry 108,399 officers and men, whose fundamental weaknesses had been exposed during the Punitive Expedition. America may have been a slumbering giant, but neither its military establishment, its people, nor its civilian industry were prepared for a major war to be fought in a foreign land more than three thousand miles from its shores. The decision to institute a Selective Service system to draft men aged eighteen to thirty-five (later raised to age forty-five) had, by the end of the war in 1918, resulted in the drafting of 2.75 million men.[32] Thus, as historian Russell F. Weigley notes, "The help that America could offer in 1917 was mostly a promise."[33]

Among the many varied and complex problems to be solved were the production and supply of weapons, uniforms, and vehicles of all sorts; the purchase of more than three hundred thousand horses and mules; the creation of training facilities; and the development and manufacture of modern weapons that would permit the U.S. Army to compete on a level playing field with the German army.[34]

For Dwight Eisenhower and other professional soldiers in the peacetime army, American entry into the war had far-reaching implications, opportunities, and disappointments. The regimental spirit that existed in the army (which has since been all but lost), decreed that an officer spend most of his career in the same regiment with which he became identified. However, to Eisenhower's intense regret, in May 1917 he was abruptly transferred to the newly forming 57th Infantry Regiment, which had no troops, no equipment, and no permanent home. To complicate matters, it was decided that the regimental bivouac and training area would be established at Leon Springs, an outpost twenty miles north of San Antonio. Situated in a dusty hellhole devoid of facilities of any kind, it meant starting from scratch to construct and staff a regimental bivouac.

The newlyweds endured their second separation and could see each other only on Sunday. For Mamie it was another manifestation of the tribulations of being an army wife whose husband was as much married to the army as he was to her. Subjected as he was to "the needs of the service," the experience of the Eisenhowers in 1917 was typical of the hardships the young couple would experience off and on throughout their marriage. The anxiety of the community of army wives who gathered in "Club Eisenhower" was not eased by the constant talk of war by their husbands or how an assignment to the AEF might be obtained. Their days playing cards or socializing with other military wives were of little comfort during the lonely nights. Their husbands never saw the tears or the loneliness. "They were, Mamie admitted afterward, the bleakest of times for her."[35] As one of her biographers has observed, "It might be military glory for the men in khaki to move in the direction of the trenches of France . . . but for their women who must wait—and hope—what could be greater torture?"[36]

The 57th Regiment was initially staffed with only a skeleton cadre from the 19th Infantry. Eisenhower's principal duty—one of the most challenging in the entire regiment—was that of regimental supply officer. On his shoulders fell the unenviable responsibility of outfitting and equipping the 3,500 men who would shortly be arriving for training. Other units were also forming, and the needs of so many new formations severely taxed the limited assets available from the Quartermaster and Ordnance Departments. Eisenhower threw himself into what would become his trademark: hard work and long hours. He solved a legion of problems with the help of an experienced supply sergeant who engaged in the army's unofficial barter system, of one hand washing another. Starting with nothing, Eisenhower and his NCO managed to beg, borrow, or trade for tentage, foodstuffs, and the other necessary essentials.

One of Eisenhower's closest friends was the regimental adjutant, Lt. Walton H. Walker, who later became one of the most aggressive corps commanders in northwestern Europe, earning him the nickname "Bulldog." Their duties brought both officers into frequent contact with the regimental commander, Col. David J. Baker, who "rewarded" them for their efficiency by assigning each a myriad of extra duties. Baker was particularly fussy about the food served in the mess hall and constantly complained that it was not to his satisfaction. Several officers had already tried to please the colonel and been dismissed before Eisenhower was given the unenviable assignment as the new mess officer. After overhearing the colonel mention how much he liked eating game, Eisenhower thought he had found a means of placating his commander. Early one morning he and Walker rode their horses to a nearby field to shoot doves, which were duly dressed and served to the finicky colonel. Unfortunately Baker became so fond of this delicacy that he pestered Eisenhower to serve game at other meals as well. Thus, Eisenhower and Walker were obliged to continue their shooting forays until the day disaster nearly struck.

Walker's regular mount was lame one morning, and he was obliged to ride a replacement horse. When he fired the first cartridge from an automatic five-shot shotgun, the horse panicked and reared uncontrollably. Then, with Walker already unable to restrain the animal, his shotgun began discharging wildly each time the horse bucked. Fearing for their lives, Eisenhower and his orderly hastily dismounted and sought refuge behind their horses. Although it could later be viewed with amusement, at the time it was another of many close calls Eisenhower would experience during his army career. On another occasion he gathered the battalion and company supply officers for a lecture when the tree under which they had sought shelter from the rain was struck by lightning. Eisenhower was knocked unconscious, and Walker, who had been on the telephone in a nearby tent, had his arm turn black and blue after nearly being fried by the electricity in the telephone line.[37]

Peacetime army promotions were so slow that it was not uncommon for it to take fifteen years or more for an officer to attain the grade of captain. In May 1917, with less than two years' service, Eisenhower was promoted to that rank.

Although Mamie had previously driven the Douds' electric car in Denver, she had never driven a gasoline-powered automobile with a standard shift. In fact, she did not even know how to start the machine or how to operate the brakes. However, if she and Ike were to see each other, Mamie made up her mind that she would have to drive the Pullman to Leon Springs. They made a date for a Sunday morning, and, as the appointed hour passed, an agitated Mamie appeared chugging down the road, shouting for Ike to jump on to the running board and *stop* the car. To avoid traffic Mamie had begun her journey near dawn by soliciting an obliging sergeant to crank the starter. Once pointed in the right direction, she somehow managed to make the entire trip to Leon Springs without braking, despite careening into a number of ditches (from which she emerged amazingly unscathed). Eisenhower often wondered how she had done it and prudently arranged for an experienced driver to accompany her whenever possible. "It was difficult to judge who was in more danger," he remarked. "The men on their way to war, or the women on their way to the men."[38] Later, whenever Eisenhower was given a rare weekend off, he hitched rides to Fort Sam on all manner of conveyances. "The trips were always through a tunnel of dust, and he was usually one of the dirtiest men on duty with Uncle Sam's Army by the time he embraced his wife."[39]

Eisenhower's experience as a supply officer left a lasting impression of the inherent perils of being accountable to the U.S. Army for its equipment. Whenever—and it was often—equipment was missing or a request went unfilled, it became Eisenhower's problem to solve. The final shipment that would complete the outfitting of the regiment was an enormous box containing carriers for the entrenching tools, an essential item for trench warfare. The regimental and battalion commanders all gathered to witness this signal event, only to discover that an outdated model had mistakenly been substituted. The box was immediately resealed and returned to the Quartermaster Department. Some months later Eisenhower was shocked to find himself billed $22.04 by the army for nineteen allegedly missing items. Despite presenting affidavits supporting his contention that nothing was taken from the shipment, Eisenhower was nevertheless held responsible for having failed to comply with a regulation requiring a complete inventory. Disgusted, he paid up, and the family budget took the hit.[40] It was his first of many disagreeable experiences with "bureaucratic blundering," and one that left him with the (mistaken) impression that in the eyes of the War Department, "I had been found wanting."[41]

The efficiency report, rendered annually or whenever an officer's principal duty is changed, is one of two powerful indicators of how far his or her career will likely advance. The other is the unofficial necessity to impress a senior officer so he will act as a mentor to help guide and promote his protégé's career. All of the high-ranking officers of World War II would have in common the support of a higher-up in a key position. However, in 1917 Eisenhower was as yet too junior to require a mentor. High praise from rating officers was a rare phenomenon, thus Eisenhower's early efficiency reports were all favorable but not particularly outstanding. For example, the endorsement by Colonel Baker in his 1917 efficiency report for his duty with the 57th Regiment rated him generally excellent in all respects but only "above the average capacity: has executive ability and considerable initiative."[42]

As the war in Europe raged on, it seemed less and less likely Eisenhower would ever be a part of it. In mid-September there was more disheartening news when he was reassigned to Fort Oglethorpe, a bleak outpost in central Georgia, where prospective officers were being trained. Although Baker endeavored to persuade the army to retain Eisenhower by substituting another captain in his place, the request was swiftly rejected. Mamie remained behind at Fort Sam to await the birth of their child, which was due at any time.

Although he later softened his recollections in his memoir, Eisenhower loathed his new duty training officer candidates, the so-called ninety-day wonders, who were needed to fill the great number of vacancies created by mobilization. Most of his days were spent in a field training area that simulated the conditions of trench warfare, including incessant rain and mud. His requests for combat duty were regularly turned down.

Except for an occasional social outing, Mamie seemed imprisoned as she awaited the birth and Ike's eventual return. With not even so much as a radio to help lighten the loneliness, her life revolved around spending many an evening knitting a garment in which the new baby would be christened. On September 24, 1917, Mamie gave birth to their first child, a son she named Doud Dwight Eisenhower. Fortunately Nana, who was recuperating in Denver from surgery, had arrived to assist her daughter. When Mamie went into labor the only transportation available was the post shuttle taxi, a medieval-looking wagon pulled by a mule, on which they hitched a ride to the infirmary. "Fort Sam Houston had no maternity facilities. 'It was no place for a mother of babies,' " Mamie later recalled. "They had to fashion a hopelessly primitive, makeshift delivery room" that was little better than a broom closet.[43] In this tiny room the birth of blond Doud Dwight Eisenhower took place so suddenly and unexpectedly that neither Nana nor the doctor were in the "delivery room" at the time. At once Mamie began calling him "Little Ike," because he bore such a striking resemblance to his father. Later this nickname was inevitably abbreviated to "Ikey" and, later still, to "Ikky."[44]

Eisenhower had barely arrived at Fort Oglethorpe when he received a telegram from his mother-in-law announcing the birth of his son. "Dearest Sweetheart," he immediately wrote to Mamie, "You could have knocked me over with a feather. Why you sweet old girl, somehow it doesn't seem possible. How I wish I could come and see you and 'IT.' . . . I'm wondering exactly what you will call the BOY. I know it will be 'Doud' for the sake of the Folks, and I think it will be fine. I hope you give him a middle name either beginning with D. or J. If it is D. then he can sign his name as D. Eisenhower, Jr., but if it is J. then it will be the same as my Dad's '*D.J.*' Anyway, I'll love the name and Him (no matter what you call him), but most of all, I'll love *YOU*. I've sent you 100,483,491,342 kisses since I've been gone." Eisenhower signed it, "Your Lover" and noted in the margin, "*YOU BET*."[45]

Ikky had his father's big hands and feet, and in his next letter Eisenhower wrote, "I'm surely glad the young scoundrel can *howl* . . . as long as it is a boy. . . . Though how in the world mother [Nana] can tell that it 'looks like us both' is more than I can see. Just wait until I get home, I'll start teaching him boxing pronto. . . . The day Mr. Young One arrived in this world his fond father was sloshing up and down the coldest, wettest, 'slipperiest' trenches in the U.S. Gee! It was awful."[46]

To no one's regret, the army abruptly closed Fort Oglethorpe in December 1917.[47] Eisenhower was ordered to Fort Leavenworth, Kansas, to embark on yet another training duty at the Army Service School. He was allowed leave to return to San Antonio to spend Christmas with Mamie and baby Doud Dwight, who became the joy of Dwight Eisenhower's life. Ikky would hang on to his father's finger, which to his proud father meant that he would surely become a football player and enter West Point.[48] For perhaps the only time during his life, Dwight Eisenhower permitted himself fully to bare his emotions. He would coo and act the clown in order to make Ikky giggle gleefully at his antics. The image of Eisenhower on his hands and knees happily uttering gibberish for Ikky's amusement was so far out of character as to be unparalleled. Other than Ida, Ikky was the only blood relative who could bring out Eisenhower's inner joy at the creation of such a beloved child and heir.

While at Fort Sam Houston he learned that a friend from the 19th Regiment was now in command of a machine-gun battalion soon to deploy overseas. Another transfer request went forward with high expectations, only to have Eisenhower's hopes dashed by yet another disapproval. To his disgust the army had clearly placed a higher value on Eisenhower's services as a training officer than in having him serve in combat. Soon after reporting to Fort Leavenworth to commence his new assignment training provisional lieutenants, Eisenhower was summoned by the post commandant and read a letter from the War Department denying his latest request for overseas duty and admonishing him for having the nerve to request it repeatedly. The place of a young officer, he was informed, was to be seen, not heard. Initiative was not only unwelcome but downright harmful to a career (another reason why Eisenhower learned never to reveal his cards in poker or to reveal his full abilities to his superiors' attention).

When the colonel added his own admonishments and suggested he ought to be punished, Eisenhower had had enough. His face turned pale with anger, and "I reverted to the old, red-necked cadet," arguing that since when was appealing for a opportunity to fight for one's country a military offense? If there was to be any punishment meted out, it must be administered by the War Department. To his surprise the colonel agreed and complimented Eisenhower for having stood up for his principles. There was no more talk of punishment.

Eisenhower knew he would probably not get another chance and that he was inexorably bound to the whims of the Washington bureaucrats. This latest incident left Eisenhower so discouraged that he never lost his contempt for deskbound staff officers who had the power to make or break his career.[49] Even in old age, Eisenhower's disgust resonated in *At Ease*, in which he wrote, "A man at a desk a thousand miles away knew better than I what my military capabilities and talents were."[50] For an officer who yearned to command troops and serve in combat, it was a substantial setback.

11.

"I . . . Will Make Up for This."

Our new Captain, Eisenhower by name, is, I believe, one of the most efficient and best army officers in the country. —LT. EDWARD C. THAYER

The winter of 1917–18 was bitterly cold, and Eisenhower was thankful for the extensive physical activity supervising bayonet training and calisthenics that at least helped ward off frostbite. He deeply missed Mamie and baby Ikky, and was utterly miserable at Fort Leavenworth performing duties he abhorred. West Point had trained him for war, but at places like Fort Oglethorpe and Fort Leavenworth, Eisenhower could hardly have been farther away from proving himself in battle. That he had little chance of escaping the repetitive training assignments rankled deeply, as did the knowledge that many of his classmates were already serving in the AEF. Worse, he was embarrassed and reckoned that to even attend a future class reunion without having served in France would be the ultimate humiliation.

Still, his success was a clear indication of his expertise as a trainer of troops. Despite his distress at being denied a chance to go overseas, during his brief tenure at Fort Leavenworth, Eisenhower made a strong impression on his charges, one of whom, Lt. Edward C. Thayer, wrote to his mother that Eisenhower "is a corker and has put more fight into us in three days than we got in all the previous time we were here. . . . He knows his job, is enthusiastic, can tell us what he wants us to do, and is pretty human, though wickedly harsh and abrupt. He has given us wonderful bayonet drills. He gets the fellows' imaginations worked up and hollers and yells and makes us shout and stomp until we go tearing into the air as if we meant business."[1] However, not everyone responded so enthusiastically to Eisenhower's brand of teaching. One of the student officers, a handsome young man named F. Scott Fitzgerald, was far more absorbed in writing his first novel, and occasionally slept through Eisenhower's lectures. Fitzgerald would later write of their mutual hostility.[2]

Eisenhower had no compassion for officers who abused their authority.

On one occasion a first lieutenant loudly berated a student in front of a group outside his office. Eisenhower summoned the lieutenant and sharply reprimanded him. As a West Point classmate who was present remembered, Eisenhower said that "no infraction could conceivably have justified the public humiliation to which this boy had been subjected. Then his voice grew kinder, but no less firm and he lectured the lieutenant on the responsibility which comes with authority. It was hardly a new idea, but Ike expressed it so eloquently yet so simply that I found myself listening as intently as the lieutenant."[3]

At the end of February 1918 his assignment to Fort Leavenworth was suddenly cut short by orders to report to Camp Meade, Maryland, an army post midway between Baltimore and Washington, D.C. Eisenhower learned that he was being assigned to an engineer unit that was organizing troops for overseas service in the newly formed Tank Corps. Excited and heartened that there might after all be a chance to participate in the war, he made a brief detour to San Antonio to see Mamie and Ikky before reporting to Camp Meade.

Early in the war the stalemate in France brought about attempts by the British to create an armored vehicle that could be used to crush the deadly barbed wire, climb up and over trenches, and advance across no-man's-land into the German trenchworks, thereby creating a breach that could be exploited by the infantry. If such a vehicle could be developed it just might turn the tide in favor of the Allies. The idea for an armored vehicle was first brought to the attention of the British War Office in October 1914 by a war correspondent who had learned of an American Holt caterpillar tractor, "which could climb like the devil."

Among the traditionalists in the British army there was scant excitement over any form of original thinking, particularly for a nonexistent mechanical monstrosity. Except, that is, for an independent-minded Englishman named Winston Churchill, the First Lord of the Admiralty. The idea held spontaneous appeal for Churchill's resourceful imagination, and he ordered his staff to get busy.[4]

By 1916 a design breakthrough occurred and a tank called "Mother" (later "Big Willie") became the first operational armored vehicle produced by the British.[5] The machine was equipped with a six-pounder gun inside a small turret, and four machine guns.[6] Although the first armored vehicles were flawed, their employment on the battlefield forever changed the course of modern warfare.[7] Forty-nine "Big Willies" participated in the Battle of the Somme, with mixed results. There was, as yet, no doctrine for their employment, and instead of massing, they were engaged individually across the front. Most broke down or became hopelessly stuck in the mud. Nevertheless several of these ungainly iron monsters were spectacularly successful, and terrorized the Germans. One led the assault on the town of Flers, which was taken without a single loss, to the cheers of the New Zealand infantry who followed them. Another straddled a trenchwork and captured three hundred German prisoners, while still another attacked a German artillery battery before being knocked out. The panic created in the front lines by these first tanks on the battlefield was reported in the German press as, "The devil is coming!"

The British painted their tanks in a variety of rainbow colors and the sight of these incredible machines may have looked comical, but they created very real alarm in the German High Command. "Secret and urgent orders were issued to German troops to hold their ground at all costs and fight to the last man against these new weapons of war."[8]

U.S. Army officer observers were interested spectators of these events, and although their reports to the War Department were disparaging of the future of the tank as a weapon of war, they nevertheless generated considerable interest in Washington and in Pershing. He established an AEF tank board, which concluded that American use of tanks was "destined to become an important element in this war," and recommended the immediate creation of a Tank Department to implement a plan to manufacture and field a force of two hundred heavy and two thousand light tanks, modeled on the British Mark VI and the Renault.[9]

In November 1917 Pershing's protégé Capt. George S. Patton became the first U.S. Army soldier to be assigned to the Tank Corps. His orders directed him to establish a tank school in Lorraine that would equip and train men in the new undertaking. At first the entire AEF Tank Corps consisted solely of Patton and a lieutenant. Yet what began without a single tank or facility would, in a matter of months, evolve into an enormous training center, which by March 1919 consisted of four hundred tanks, and five thousand tank officers and enlisted men.

As the AEF and the War Department grappled with the immense problem of creating, staffing, training, and deploying a tank service that had not only never been tested in battle but which lacked tanks, several tank training centers were rapidly established in the United States to begin training additional troops for future deployment to France and service in the AEF.

The headquarters of the new U.S. Tank Corps evolved from the former engineer unit at Camp Meade and was mainly responsible for training and deploying troops and formations for service in the AEF Tank Corps. Its first director was Lt. Col. Ira C. Welborn, an infantry officer who had won the Medal of Honor during the Spanish-American War. Based in Washington, Welborn was primarily an administrator who coordinated the recruitment of volunteers, rather than a commander.[10] But, as historian Dale Wilson notes in his landmark account of the birth of the Tank Corps, there were no tanks yet available to train in, nor was there even any contact with the AEF Tank

Corps. "It was, in effect, a Tank Corps in name only. Each of the Corps's training centers provided little more than basic soldier training . . . actual combat training would have to wait until units deployed to France."[11]

At Camp Meade, Eisenhower quickly put his training experience to good use and made a strong first impression upon his superiors by helping to organize, train, and equip an all-volunteer unit designated the 301st Tank Battalion. Eisenhower believed that it was only a matter of time before the 301st deployed overseas, and in mid-March he learned that not only was the 301st being sent to France, but that he would be its commander. Ecstatic that his luck had finally turned, Eisenhower rushed to New York to coordinate the sailing of the 301st to France. His attention to the smallest detail and seemingly endless questions annoyed the Port of New York authorities, but Eisenhower was determined that nothing untoward occur to mar the timely sailing of his battalion.

At the last moment, however, Eisenhower's hopes were dashed when he was informed that instead of leading the 301st to France, he was being reassigned to command a temporary military garrison adjacent to the Gettysburg battlefield: Camp Colt. Eisenhower's organizational abilities had convinced his superiors that he was more valuable training troops. The curse of being a successful troop trainer had struck again, and "My mood was black," he said.[12] His new assignment was a perfect example of the military axiom "For the good of the service." Eisenhower's method of coping was to vent his frustrations in private. "Whenever I had convinced myself that my superiors, through bureaucratic oversights . . . had doomed me to run-of-the-mill assignments, I found no better cure than to blow off steam in private and then settle down to the job at hand."[13]

Near the site of Pickett's charge, Eisenhower established and commanded the largest tank-training center in the United States so impressively that he was promoted from captain to lieutenant colonel in seven months.[14] Eisenhower arrived at Camp Colt on March 24, 1918, with a small cadre and hoisted the American flag on the camp flagpole. He replaced an older former NCO named Garner, who had been promoted to captain in 1917. After the brief ceremony, "with tears steaming down his face," Garner related how he had once been court-martialed at Camp Colt and ironically was now the temporary commander at the site of his disgrace. This event left a permanent mark on Eisenhower, who never again saluted a flag without thinking with compassion of the older officer.[15]

Situated inside the Gettysburg National Park, Camp Colt was first occupied in 1917, then enlarged the following year to accommodate four thousand men.[16] The place was crude and lacked even the most basic amenities, including stoves in the tents. In April 1918 a blizzard buried the camp and Eisenhower trudged through the snowdrifts to Gettysburg, where he purchased every available stove he could locate. Such was the state of the U.S. military that even this stopgap measure did not fulfill his requirements. Frequently during his tenure at Camp Colt, Eisenhower was hampered by army red tape that further affirmed his aversion to bureaucrats. Fortunately there were only about five hundred men in Camp Colt at the time, or the results might have been far more serious.

Gettysburg was a place that possessed a special attraction for Eisenhower. He was intimately knowledgeable about every aspect of the desperate battles fought there in July 1863, both from a battlefield tour in 1915 while still at West Point, and from his extensive reading. Of all the campaigns and battles Eisenhower studied in his lifetime, none intrigued him more than Gettysburg. He felt deeply for the men of the Confederacy who were so needlessly slaughtered there and, years later, as Allied supreme commander in Europe, he empathized with and drew strength from the loneliness of command and the trials of the Union commander, Gen. George Meade. As he had at West Point, where he roamed the academy grounds, Eisenhower found solace tramping the battlefield alone whenever he could spare some time for himself. Later on, when Mamie arrived, he would take her to the various battlefield sites and explain the events that had taken place there. Even though it was not a subject that particularly interested her, Mamie was proud that her husband was so knowledgeable that he "knew every rock of that battlefield."

Eisenhower was in his element at Camp Colt. His work was manly, rewarding, and challenging. The ultimate rewards were promotion and, if his luck held, perhaps a chance to test himself in battle. Those who served there soon learned that their new commanding officer was a strict disciplinarian with a terrible temper that, when triggered, often caused its recipients literally to quake in their boots. Soldiers who chafed under Patton's strict observance of high standards and attention to detail would have found no consolation in Eisenhower's command of Camp Colt. He believed that high morale is obtained through exacting standards of discipline, and weathered demands from politicians who attempted to influence him on behalf of a constituent. Eisenhower demanded—and won—unquestioning obedience from his officers and men. The tent city grew explosively as additional units were organized and new recruits flooded in during the summer of 1918. Eventually Camp Colt became both a mobilization and training center. Although its capacity was 4,000, by midsummer 1918, 10,600 troops had been assigned there.

Eisenhower's favorable impression on his superiors brought rapid promotions, first to temporary major in June 1918, and then to temporary lieutenant colonel in mid-October, on his twenty-eighth birthday. For an officer with less than three years' commissioned service, the responsibilities he was given in 1918 were a sure sign of his professional competence.[17]

An essential element of any successful command is to forge a strong first impression. Although Eisenhower was only a very junior captain when he took over, there was never the slightest doubt who was in charge of Camp Colt. He exerted his will in a number of ways that gained the respect of the new tank men, who were reassured that they were serving under an outstanding officer who cared about them as individuals. Those who failed to live up to his standards were shown no mercy. Discipline was severe, and Eisenhower its eager administrator. Violators of army and camp regulations were swiftly punished. Throughout his military career, Eisenhower had no toleration for yes-men and once was heard to berate a lieutenant: "I want you to figure out some things which are wrong with this camp. You make me uncomfortable by always agreeing with me . . . you either don't say what you think, or you are as big a fool as I am!"[18]

After one of his junior officers was caught cheating with a marked deck of playing cards, an unforgiving Eisenhower offered him a simple choice: Resign or face a court-martial. The officer resigned, but his father complained to his congressman. Several days later the father and the politician arrived to attempt to persuade Eisenhower to cancel the resignation and transfer the man to another post. When Eisenhower refused, pointing out that he would not send an unfit officer to another command where he would repeat his bad behavior, the congressman suggested he amend the discharge to read, "For the good of the service." Eisenhower again declined, and the two left empty-handed.[19]

Despite his enthusiasm and organizational abilities, Eisenhower could not overcome the lack of tank doctrine and equipment with which to train his recruits. Reduced to a superficial form of basic training and parade-ground drill and ceremonies, the "Treat 'Em Rough" Boys, as the men of the Tank Corps became known, were soldiers without a mission.

A camp newspaper, created in May 1918, also called *Treat 'Em Rough,* served as a morale builder by offering news of interest. Poetry, which was very popular during the war, also appeared. One of World War I's oddities was the mournful singing by German soldiers and British Tommies across no-man's-land during the spontaneous Christmas truce of 1914. Americans had their own nationalistic songs such as "Over There," but the rebel yells of the Civil War had progressed to songs praising the Doughboy of World War I. Anxious for an identity, the soldiers of the new tank service invented their own limericks and songs, which Eisenhower avidly supported, as much for his love of singing (which he still did quite badly) as for their effect as a morale builder.[20] One of the most original poems was called "We'll All Tank Together Over There." An example:

> It takes the good old tank boys
> To show them the way;
> To win the town to-day.

You talk about your infantry,
Your blooming engineers,
But they'll never beat the tanks
In a hundred thousand years.

. . . It takes the good old tank boys
To beat the dirty Hun;
It takes the good old tank boys
To keep them on the run.
They've got the giant Zeppelin,
The cruel submarine,
But we'll grease their road to hell, boys,
With oleomargarine.

(Refrain)
We'll all tank together over there, boys,
We'll all tank together over there, boys,
Some will go to heaven
Some will go to hell,
But we'll all tank together over there, boys.[21]

The possession or consumption of alcohol was forbidden, and nearby Gettysburg and several other small towns became meccas for thirsty soldiers in search of refreshment while on pass. In spite of the troops' generally favorable acceptance by the local people, a growing number of incidents involving Eisenhower's men brought complaints of bad behavior, drunkenness, and brawling. The other side of the coin was that some civilian establishments preyed on soldiers. Under War Department regulations, local commanders were given the authority to place off-limits any local establishment serving liquor. Rather than encourage a black market in bootleg booze, Eisenhower requested that saloonkeepers regulate themselves by voluntarily refraining from catering to soldiers in uniform. The alternative, he said, was the imposition of an off-limits edict. Most complied, but one Gettysburg hotel, although not technically a saloon, covertly continued to sell liquor until the day Eisenhower ordered his provost marshal to surround the establishment with military police, thus effectively cutting off business not just to his soldiers but to visiting civilians.

After promising to comply, the owner reneged and the MPs returned. The irate owner obtained the assistance of the local congressman, both men expecting that Eisenhower, then a mere major, would be sufficiently intimidated to acquiesce. The congressman's crude threat, "We have means—we can go to the War Department. If you're going to be so stubborn, I'll have to take up the question of replacing you," was met by the full fury of Eisenhower's monumental temper and his refusal to be unnerved by a mere politician. "You do just exactly that," he angrily retorted. "Nothing would please me better than to be taken out of this job. I want to go overseas. If they take me out of here, maybe I can get there."[22] A complaint was duly filed but was strongly rebuffed by the War Department. Rather than be relieved of command, Eisenhower received a letter of commendation from the assistant secretary of war, conveying Secretary of War Newton D. Baker's compliments for his diligence in safekeeping the welfare of his troops.[23] His run-ins with conniving politicians while at Camp Colt merely reinforced what West Point had instilled in him: that politicians were a despicable lot. Yet it would prove to have been good experience for what lay two decades ahead.

The Tank Corps was expected to find and commission officers from within its own ranks, and Eisenhower used this as a motivational tool, writing in a formal letter that one "who shows in his appearance that he has the proper pride in himself, the Tank Corps, and the Army, has a big start toward a commission."[24] The troops assigned to Camp Colt were organized into tank battalions, which eventually grew in number to five tank regiments, twenty-seven tank battalions, and units from four divisions, all of which trained there under Eisenhower's command, and many of which were subsequently deployed to the AEF.[25]

Training raw recruits was a great challenge. Camp Colt and army general orders had to be memorized, then practiced while on guard duty. His tankless units were formed so quickly that some were commanded by junior officers as low in grade as first lieutenant. One of these was 2nd Lt. Floyd Parks, who made such an outstanding impression on his commander that in short order he was given command of a battalion. The two never lost contact with each other after the war, and for the rest of his life Eisenhower counted Parks, who eventually rose to the rank of lieutenant general, as one of his dearest friends.

As volunteers, the men who made up the Tank Corps were generally a cut above the World War I level of recruit, better educated and high spirited. The problem was finding sufficient activities to keep them interested and involved. Although he knew next to nothing about tanks or their employment, Eisenhower wrote in "A Message to the Men," in July 1918, that they were an elite group who would have to learn not only how to employ tanks on a battlefield but work in full cooperation with the three basic branches of the army: the infantry, cavalry, and artillery. "We read on our poster—'Why walk to Berlin when you can ride in a tank?' . . . we have here in Camp Colt one of the finest collections of men and officers anywhere in our army." The memo was typically Eisenhower in its combination of praise and exhortation. "[T]he Tank Corps," he wrote, "although the baby branch of the service, is a baby only in name—perhaps a baby wild cat—and the slogan 'Treat 'Em Rough' will prove to be a very appreciative phrase when the kitten has grown a bit more and sharpened his claws for the Boche."[26] Recruiting posters depicted a vicious-looking black cat with sharp teeth and formidable claws, above which was written TREAT 'EM ROUGH! Below, there appeared underneath a group of tanks the words JOIN THE TANKS, UNITED STATES TANK CORPS.

Like everyone else in the Tank Corps in the United States, including Welborn, Eisenhower was completely unaware of the tank activity in France. His future friend George S. Patton was busily rounding the AEF Tank Corps into a first-class fighting force that would in September and October 1918 distinguish itself during the Saint-Mihiel offensive and the Meuse-Argonne campaign.

Although no one expected there would be any tanks to train with in the United States, in June 1918, a Renault light tank, the same machine used by the AEF Tank Corps and the first anyone in America had ever seen, was delivered to Camp Colt. The troops reacted to this signal event with what Eisenhower called "cheerful cynicism" at finally being able to actually train on a real tank. Eventually Camp Colt received two additional tanks, along with two British tank officer advisers. Unfortunately one of the most important aspects of tank training vanished when it was learned that the Renaults had been sent without their armaments. Once again, as was so often the case during the war, training centers such as Camp Colt were reduced to "simulation," a term that really meant teaching theory and making believe. Although Camp Colt lacked the necessary equipment to fully prepare men for battle in France, it did not lack for initiative and ingenuity, both of which Eisenhower prized. He and his staff resorted to every means they could think of to sustain morale and improve training, including scouring books, magazines, and military manuals for ideas that might have application to tank training.

His frequent letters, speeches, and memos to his troops were a forerunner of the wealth of such missives penned by Eisenhower during World War II. Some, like the intense and melodramatic speech called "Our Flag," which he delivered on the activation of a tank battalion, praised the flag and all it stood for: duty and the "great honor" they had been given of fighting for the United States. "Together with millions of others of America's Best, you have arisen to defiantly shout IT SHALL BE DONE, and now you are offering your lives to prove your words . . . as you go forth to take your part in this greatest war . . . may this flag sustain you."[27] It may have been theatrical but it helped achieve the high morale Eisenhower sought. Even more relevant was the fact that the cynical West Point cadet of 1911–15 had, by 1918, matured into both a patriot and an ambitious and dedicated career army officer.

Mamie's transition from San Antonio to Gettysburg required a difficult and exhausting four-day rail journey. Seven-month-old Ikky was ill with a fever that was a prelude to the chicken pox, when they arrived inauspiciously in the snow and freezing temperatures of the storm of April 1918. The frustrating journey ended on a disagreeable note when Eisenhower failed to turn up at the railroad station. Mamie was met instead by one of his men who explained that Captain Eisenhower was busy dealing with the problem of obtaining heaters for his frozen troops.

Mamie had never made a move to another place army-style, much less by herself. There are few secrets in a tight-knit military community, and word quickly spread that Mamie would shortly be leaving for Gettysburg to join her husband. An older, neighboring army wife appeared at her door and asked Mamie what she planned to do with her furniture and household goods, noting that any experienced army family avoided the hassle of moving by selling them, then buying new items at the next post. Naturally, the woman said, she would be quite willing to take them all off Mamie's hands for a fair price. To her great regret, Mamie fell for this ruse and received only ninety dollars for virtually everything in the family quarters except for a rug, linens, and personal items. The army had prohibited the wearing of civilian clothes off duty, which became Mamie's rationale for getting rid of Ike's two custom-made double-breasted suits, which he loved but she thought were "horrid eyesores." They cost three hundred dollars and were sold to a rag man for ten dollars. Mamie ill-advisedly believed Ike would not miss them until after the war. However, as soon as he began unpacking their trunks in Gettysburg, Eisenhower began searching in vain for his suits, at which point Mamie was obliged to admit what she had done. Eisenhower's monumental temper erupted in brief outrage. Recalled Mamie, "The suit episode was enough to unsettle a saint." Although he quickly dropped the matter, "he told her he hoped she'd grow up and learn a true sense of values, a remark which hurt more than his anger." Left unspoken was the small matter of the pittance she had received for their household items. Her husband never asked, and she never volunteered an explanation. "How could I have been so gullible?" Mamie later wondered. "I know I was young, but not *that* young . . . what I exchanged for nine $10 bills cost originally over $900." Her carefully guarded savings took a severe hit, and it was not until years later that she told Ike the truth.[28]

Military quarters were either nonexistent or difficult to secure. The first of the Eisenhowers' three domiciles in Gettysburg was a dank, evil-smelling, two-story frame house of microscopic size. The only heat came from a coal stove that Eisenhower had to show Mamie how to operate. She remembered, "It *was* a very difficult time for me . . . at home [in Denver] the cook would not allow us in the kitchen, so I never had any kitchen experience at all." During the summer of 1918, they moved into much roomier accommodations in a large fraternity house at Gettysburg College, which lacked a kitchen. "Ike had a chef . . . in his headquarters company. No wonder he'd go and eat at camp—and take me."[29]

Eisenhower was rarely home and thus unable to spend much time with his family. What precious little free time he did have was typically spent playing with or holding his small son. More often, however, he could be found prowling around the camp at all hours, checking up, asking questions, and using his presence to signal the importance of the training. One day Mamie jokingly suggested that perhaps she could have a ride in one of Ike's steel contraptions. He happily acceded, and Mamie got the ride of her life one evening as her husband drove a Renault tank, at bone-jarring speeds, through a ditch, in reverse, and through the equivalent of modern-day "wheelies." The crude roar of the engine ringing in her ears, the eye-watering, pungent odor of gasoline, and clouds of choking dust combined to make her one and only venture into her husband's work arena memorable. Secretly Mamie was proud of her feat, particularly inasmuch as she knew she was likely to be the first woman ever to have ridden in a tank.[30]

In September 1918 Eisenhower's earlier problems were dwarfed by comparison with one of the gravest challenges he ever faced. Camp Colt's population had swelled to more than ten thousand men when Eisenhower suddenly had to employ every skill he possessed to contain a threat far more deadly than the world war then in progress. Dubbed the "Spanish flu," it was a deadly and particularly virulent outbreak of biblical proportions that spread throughout the world and hit the United States like a hurricane. Although the true numbers will never be known, the 1918 virus killed an estimated 548,000 Americans. Nothing like it had been seen before (or has been since). Overnight the profession of undertaking became a growth industry. Worldwide, an estimated 20 to 100 million people died rapid and horrible deaths from this plague that was twenty-five times more deadly than so-called ordinary flu. The U.S. Army was not spared; indeed, the frequent movement of troops from place to place helped spread the virus, which was eventually contracted by more than one-third of its members. Before it ended, the average life expectancy in the United States had dropped by a staggering twelve years.[31]

The camp surgeon, Lt. Col. Thomas Scott, initially misdiagnosed the suddenly growing numbers of sick soldiers before realizing his mistake and quarantining the infected in segregated areas of the camp. All manner of inoculations were tried, and each failed. Men began dying (literally overnight), and a grave problem became, in Eisenhower's words, "a nightmare," which spread to the town of Gettysburg. As lines grew outside the hospital, there was no place to store the dead and no coffins in which to place them. A mounting sense of fear pervaded Camp Colt. (One soldier who was thought to have died was moved to a makeshift morgue and laid out naked with the other dead. Later, as his comrades filed by to pay their last respects, the man awoke and exclaimed, "Get me out of here!" The men were so unnerved by this bizarre incident that they stampeded from the tent and into the site of Pickett's charge, taking with them the troops awaiting inoculations intended to prevent an outbreak of other diseases, such as smallpox and typhoid.) When his medics ran out of space, Eisenhower arranged to have the overflow sent to a parochial school in Gettysburg and to local churches, which were turned into makeshift hospitals.

The medical staff acted aggressively to isolate the sick from the rest of the camp. Inoculations and daily examinations were ordered. Even as he was coping with the epidemic, Eisenhower feared for his family's safety. Dr. Scott concocted two homemade nasal and throat sprays that he tried out on Eisenhower, his staff, and Mamie, one of which was so noxious that Eisenhower thought the top of his head would blow off each time it was administered twice daily. Whether or not the remedy worked is unknown, but no one who used the spray became ill. Although the epidemic was contained in about a week, before the crisis passed there were 150 deaths from the Spanish flu at Camp Colt. Compared with responses at other military facilities, the actions taken by Eisenhower and his medical staff at Camp Colt were so efficient that the War Department ordered him to send thirty of his physicians to other installations to train their medical personnel.

Although mass fatalities were avoided within the U.S. military, the Spanish flu and pneumonia killed more military men (52,019) than were killed in combat (50,475). Eisenhower never forgot the contributions of his chief surgeon, noting in his memoir that Scott was "another of those men to whom I will always feel obligated."[32]

Rumors of a possible armistice in Europe began reaching Gettysburg about the time a telegram from Denver left Mamie thunderstruck. Her beloved younger sister Buster had died suddenly at age seventeen. Buster was the second of Mamie's sisters to die in childhood (and at the same age as Mamie's older sister, Eleanor).[33] After Ike and Mamie bade each other a tearful good-bye in Harrisburg, Eisenhower sent Elvira Doud a poignant condolence letter. "My Own Dearest Mother," he wrote, ". . . we are heartbroken. . . . We can feel *your* grief. . . . I cannot come—duty prevents—but even now I know that the love you bear your children tells you that my heart and my love are with you."[34]

Colonel Welborn had assured Eisenhower that he would be permitted to deploy to France in command of a tank regiment, and, adding to Mamie's anxiety, she left Gettysburg fully expecting that she might not see him again. The death of Buster was difficult enough; now she also had to contend with her husband's imminent departure for France and the unknown terrors that face all families with loved ones placed in harm's way. Even so, Welborn attempted to dissuade Eisenhower from going to France by dangling the promise of an immediate promotion to full colonel, an offer he flatly rejected.

So anxious was Eisenhower to achieve his ambition that he made it known he would, if need be, cheerfully accept a reduction in rank to major, "if the lieutenant colonelcy which I have now stands in the way of my going overseas."[35]

His promotion to lieutenant colonel turned out to be a short-lived source of pride. By the time Mamie and Ikky reached Denver the war had ended, with rejoicing all across the United States. And, while the announcement of the armistice on the Western Front that brought to a conclusion the most terrible war in the history of mankind, on the eleventh hour of the eleventh day of the eleventh month of 1918, brought a sense of relief to Mamie, it thoroughly dismayed her husband.

A frustrated Eisenhower angrily remarked to his classmate Norman Randolph, "I suppose we'll spend the rest of our lives explaining why we didn't get into this war. By God, from now on I am cutting myself a swath and will make up for this."[36]

To have missed such an opportunity was not only dismaying but potentially career killing. His friend and classmate Omar Bradley had likewise seen no overseas duty during the war; instead he was placed in command of a security force sent to guard the Anaconda copper mines in Butte, Montana, against strikers and agitators thought to be anarchists. Bradley's disappointment mirrored Eisenhower's. Proclaiming it "professionally, the most frustrating [event] of my early Army career," Bradley described how "my overwhelming desire at that time was to go to France and prove my mettle in a real war. . . . I tried every possible scheme I could dream up . . . [to join] an outfit bound for France."[37]

So it was that instead of going off to war, Eisenhower was ordered to disband Camp Colt, and by December 1918 the once-sprawling complex once again resembled a graveyard. The dreary period between the armistice and demobilization proved to be the greatest hurdle he had to overcome as camp commander. Nothing he had learned at West Point or during his three years of service had prepared him for the challenge of demobilization on a truly massive scale. Suddenly there was little to do other than unnecessary training ("ridiculous," he called it) or make-work projects that Eisenhower deemed "self-defeating." He was all too aware that, "No human enterprise goes flat so instantly as an Army training camp when war ends."[38] Housekeeping details were tightened, and Eisenhower dangled the lure of imminent discharges in exchange for patience. Most cooperated, in no small part because of his persuasiveness.

Most of those still remaining at Camp Colt were moved in December 1918 to Camp Dix, New Jersey, for discharge from the mobilization that had seen the U.S. Army expand to 2,395,742 officers and men earlier in the same year. The Tank Corps likewise had grown from nothing in early 1918 to 1,275 officers and 18,977 enlisted men by November. By December fewer than 6,000 men remained at Camp Colt. The move itself, logistically complicated, turned out to be Eisenhower's final act as camp commander.

Shortly after the armistice was declared, another classmate, Maj. Philip K. McNair, encountered Eisenhower on a train. "He was greatly upset. He hadn't been sent overseas and now he never would be. He said he had been educated to be a soldier, and when a war came along, he had to sit it out without even getting close to the battle. He was so keenly disappointed. . . . I had the definite impression that he intended on resigning his commission. I was sure he and the Army were through."[39]

For all his frustrations and fears about his professional future, Eisenhower had performed admirably in a very difficult job that won him many admirers. As historian Dale Wilson sums up Ike's Camp Colt experience, "He had excelled in every way, showing great ingenuity in developing a meaningful training program despite the lack of resources. He had also shown a great deal of skill in dealing with politicians and community and business leaders," as well as with the two British liaison officers, with whom he had worked well.[40] For his service at Camp Colt, Welborn recommended Eisenhower for the Distinguished Service Medal, the army's highest peacetime decoration, but the army bounced the recommendation around until 1924, when it was finally approved. Welborn's esteem for his subordinate was also noted on Eisenhower's efficiency report. As a captain Eisenhower had performed duties equivalent to those of a brigadier general. "I regard this officer as one of the most efficient young officers I have known," Welborn wrote.[41]

During the rush to return soldiers to civilian life, an appeal was made to induce enough men to form the nucleus of a postwar Tank Corps to remain on active duty. Several hundred accepted, and both Eisenhower and his volunteers were ordered to report to Fort Benning, Georgia, the home of the infantry. The rail journey to Georgia was hellish. The train was constantly shuttled onto sidings for higher-priority movements. Even low-flying birds, mused Eisenhower, seemed to move faster and have a higher precedence. There was no kitchen, no lights, no heat, and no hot water, though Eisenhower managed to fashion a crude kitchen of sorts in the baggage car, using portable stoves. His own World War I could not have ended on a more ignominious note.[42] For all his success as a trainer and troop commander, Eisenhower's future remained clouded as the United States approached the decade of the Roaring Twenties, during which its armed forces all but vanished.

12.

"A Journey Through Darkest America"

I wanted to go along partly for a lark and partly to learn.

After Buster's funeral Mamie remained in Denver while the army pondered the future of the Tank Corps. Nearly a year would elapse before Ike and Mamie were reunited. The move to Fort Benning was temporary, and, with little to do in the euphoric aftermath of the armistice, Eisenhower had "far too much time on my hands." In March 1919 he was delighted to receive orders to return to Camp Meade, which had been selected as the permanent home of the Tank Corps. When re-formed, the Tank Corps consisted of units from the United States and the AEF, under the command of Brig. Gen. Samuel D. Rockenbach, a cavalry officer and the director of the AEF Tank Corps, who took over from Ira Welborn in August 1919. Rockenbach, an officer "famous for his razor-edged tongue and his martinet ship," was Patton's boss in France. Rockenbach often exasperated him by what Patton perceived as foot dragging in the acquisition of the first tanks for the AEF Tank Corps, once privately calling him "a good hearted wind bag." Despite their differences and the occasional dust-up, Rockenbach stoutly defended Patton and generally avoided interfering. Rockenbach's wife, a noted horsewoman, when once asked why she had married "Rocky," replied, "I married him for his conformation, of course. Did you ever see a finer piece of man-flesh?"[1] Eisenhower was never enamored of Rockenbach, because of his new commander's direct order that he coach the Camp Meade football team. Eisenhower mistakenly thought that, as a senior officer in the Tank Corps, he had advanced to the point where coaching was no longer a career necessity. Rockenbach quickly disabused him of this notion, and Eisenhower had the good sense not to protest the assignment further. With his usual verve and leadership, Eisenhower successfully coached the Tank School football team from 1919 to 1921, for which he received a glowing letter of commendation from Rockenbach for his "splendid efforts."

. . .

In the aftermath of the war, pressure began mounting for Eisenhower to leave the army. One of his junior officers at Camp Colt failed to tempt him to accept employment with his firm in Indiana at a considerably higher salary. Mamie observed, "A lot of his classmates were getting out and they had big positions with this firm and that. The next thing I knew they were working on Ike to get him out of the service." Despite the wretched pay and lack of amenities, however, Eisenhower was simply not prepared to give up his career for the humdrum existence and the uncertainties of civilian life. Tempted as he may have been, he knew that military life suited him well, and even Mamie, who might have been expected to endorse the stability of civilian life, had matured to the point where she advised her husband not to leave the army. "I said to him—it was about only twice that I remember that I really interfered—and this time I said, 'Well, Ike, I don't think you'd be happy. This is your life and you know it and you like it. Now true, there's not any money in it, but we have other personal things that make up for the lack of currency . . . so I talked him into staying."[2]

The decision proved fortuitous. "I knew no matter what I said he was going to make his own decision" as the head of the family. "My father cracked the whip around the house, and I tell you everybody paid attention to Mr. Doud. I never felt like I had to help Ike in any way, except in making as nice a family-life as possible. I thought he was perfectly capable of paddling his own canoe. It just never occurred to me to give him any advice on his business."[3]

The perks of army life and the kinship of the brotherhood of the officer corps proved to be a greater enticement to Eisenhower. Moreover, there would always be a steady paycheck each month from the government, a point underscored when the country sank into the depths of the Great Depression. Despite obvious relief that Ike was out of harm's way, Mamie shared his disappointment at not having gone overseas. "I felt so sorry for him. . . . After all this career that he'd worked so hard for, and he thought so much of, he just didn't think there was going to be any solution," after trying so hard and failing to see action in France.

At Camp Meade, Eisenhower was back on familiar ground working with the Tank Corps, although initially in a paper-shuffling job. In 1919 Meade was a major demobilization point as the army grappled with the problem of reducing its massive troop strength to a peacetime level. Despite a heavy workload, and on their own initiative, Eisenhower and several colleagues managed to find time to organize and teach a night school for aspiring Regular Army officers in such subjects as tactics, math, history, and English.

Also in March 1919 the remnants of the AEF Tank Corps, led by Col. George S. Patton, returned from France to the United States and Camp

Meade, their final destination. Patton retained command of the 304th Tank Brigade, which he had trained and commanded in France. Soon afterward, however, Patton left for detached service in Washington as a member of a Tank Board charged with writing formal army doctrine and the necessary military manuals governing the operation of tank units. The very survival of the Tank Corps was already in question, and its future depended on establishing it as a necessary arm of the army in a future war. While Patton was away Eisenhower was given temporary command of the 304th. The two officers had yet to meet each other. All Patton knew was that an unknown lieutenant colonel named Eisenhower was standing in for him.

In 1919 there was no such thing as a highway system in the United States. Most roads were still dirt, and where they even existed they were poorly constructed, dangerous, and all but impassable in bad weather—facts that were not lost on the War Department, which had experienced serious problems attempting to move units and equipment by road during the war. At the instigation of a bright young officer who perceived the public relations value of such a venture, the War Department decided to create a transcontinental motor expedition, whereby a convoy of eighty-one assorted U.S. Army vehicles would attempt to cross the continental United States, no mean feat in 1919.

"The 1919 transcontinental convoy had a Homeric flavor to it. The internal combustion engine was still in its infancy and was not as dependable as it is today. A transcontinental convoy had never been attempted before and the army, in fact, was not sure that it could be done."[4] A journey by road in 1919, when the railroad was still supreme and some so-called roads were little more than cart tracks or trails carved out of the wilderness, was truly an adventure not to be undertaken lightly.

The section of Camp Meade assigned to the tank men had no married quarters, thus Mamie was still in Denver and not likely to be joining him for the foreseeable future. Eisenhower was bored to tears and thirsting for adventure, anything to escape the humdrum existence of the peacetime army. When he learned of the proposed expedition, Eisenhower immediately volunteered and was accepted as a Tank Corps observer, "partly for a lark and partly to learn."

At his recommendation Eisenhower was joined by a second Tank Corps observer, Maj. Sereno E. Brett, a veteran tank officer who had commanded a battalion with distinction under Patton in the Meuse-Argonne. Next to Patton, Brett was regarded as the most aggressive tank commander in the entire AEF and was an officer Patton held in high esteem. After Patton was severely wounded during the first day of the Meuse-Argonne campaign, Brett assumed command of his 1st Tank Brigade for the remainder of the war, fighting until all that was left were a handful of men and tanks. Patton recommended

Brett for the Distinguished Service Cross and wrote a heartfelt letter, "putting in writing what I have long felt in my heart. . . . As far as I know no officer of the AEF has given more faithful, loyal, and gallant service."[5] Like Eisenhower, Brett had opted to remain in the service after the war and was also assigned to Camp Meade, where he and Eisenhower became friends. Brett was outgoing and great company, and from him Eisenhower learned what he had missed by not having been a participant in the AEF Tank Corps. Both were sufficiently bored with garrison duty to volunteer immediately for the expedition.

The expedition departed Washington, D.C., on July 7, 1919, bound for San Francisco, 3,251 miles away. Their orders arrived too late for Eisenhower and Brett to attend the official send-off in Washington, held at the Zero Milestone marker, situated not far from the White House. In attendance at the typically Washingtonian ceremony were a host of VIPs, including Secretary of War Newton Baker, U.S. Army Chief of Staff Peyton C. March, and a bevy of politicians. There were the usual long-winded speeches, about which Eisenhower later gleefully noted, "My luck was running; we missed the ceremony."[6] The two officers caught up with the convoy in Frederick, Maryland, the first night.

To add realism to the expedition, the convoy operated under simulated wartime conditions as a motor march through enemy territory. The convoy consisted of army vehicles, some with solid rubber tires, others with pneumatic tires. In addition to some sixty trucks (two of which had been turned into makeshift ambulances), there were also motorcycles (some with sidecars), staff cars, a powerful van-mounted searchlight, a tank transported on a flatbed trailer, and various other trailers used as mobile kitchens and repair shops. The expedition was sponsored in part by several of the major automobile manufacturers, including Willys, Packard, Mack, and General Motors. Willys sent several "mystery cars," which were prototype models not yet available to the public. The lead truck was emblazoned with the words WE'RE OFF TO FRISCO!

Overall the expedition consisted of 24 officers, 258 enlisted men, some two dozen War Department observers, and numerous others who tagged along for parts of the journey, as well as reporters and representatives of auto and tire manufacturers. Officially its mission was "to test various military vehicles, many developed too late for use in World War I, and to determine by actual experience the feasibility of moving an army across the continent."[7]

The trip also served as a selling point for the military. At virtually every stop, curious townspeople across the country ventured out to view the expedition and hear speeches about its purpose, and the members of the expedition were royally received. "Almost every town in the vicinity of the route of travel, and the nightly encampments, would provide some social activity as well as food and drink. These events ranged from dances and banquets, to melon feeds, and outdoor movies."[8] The official report of the expedition stated that the meals produced by the mobile mess were dreadful at the start but improved partway through the journey, after the officer in charge was replaced. An experienced army engineer, Master Sgt. Harry C. DeMars, had a different recollection. Shortly after the trip commenced, the mess truck was "left behind, as so many organizations were preparing meals for them when they entered the various towns. When crossing the desert, meals were brought to them. The soldiers stopped at Y.M.C.A.s to take baths." Most of the men slept on cots outside their vehicles, but sleep remained at a premium; "Townspeople would mill through the camp all night."[9] In Sacramento the governor lauded them as akin to the "Immortal Forty-Niners." There were also seemingly endless speeches by VIPs, which severely tested Eisenhower's capacity for enduring pompous rhetoric.

In the tradition of the expeditions that opened the western United States, the motorcycles were ridden by scouts, whose task it was to investigate road conditions and, with road signs generally lacking, determine the convoy's route. To gain an idea of the hardships of crossing the United States, the convoy averaged fifty-eight miles per day at an average speed of six miles per hour.

The realism of this pioneering journey hardly needed the simulation of wartime conditions. Traveling across the United States in 1919 was a major feat in itself. "For the next two months, through rain, mud and searing heat of summer on the western plains and deserts, Eisenhower and Brett learned firsthand why America needed a transcontinental system of highways."[10]

One of the most instrumental members of the expedition was a civilian ordnance technician from Raritan Arsenal, New Jersey, Edwin A. Reis, "who was given high praise for the success of the convoy for he frequently was the only person who could figure out what to do when vehicles broke down or were totally mired."[11] Indeed, Murphy's law was in full force over the course of the expedition. Vehicles broke down with regularity, became stuck in the mud or quicksand, sank when the roads collapsed beneath them, or absorbed enormous quantities of choking dust. A truck sped out of control down a Pennsylvania mountain, tires shredded, ignitions failed, engines died, vehicles slid off the roads into ditches and gullies, and in Utah some broke through the salt flats. Remarkably, however, the expedition lost only a handful of vehicles that could not be repaired.

Wyoming was particularly difficult. Most of the bridges were too light to cross with the expedition's five-ton vehicles and had to be either replaced or jury-rigged. Sometimes both a truck and the tractor attempting to pull it out sank into the mud, necessitating Herculean efforts by the engineers to recover them. Often roads had to be constructed or rebuilt in places. Some days the expedition averaged only a few miles. Overall the engineers rebuilt or modified sixty-two bridges between Washington and San Francisco.

Although Eisenhower thought discipline was far too lax, he and Brett enjoyed a carefree interlude with few responsibilities and ample time for fun. The same prankish Eisenhower who delighted in pouring buckets of water on unsuspecting victims at West Point resurfaced during the expedition. Each perhaps spurred on by the other, both men became first-rate pranksters who relished frightening the citified easterners who made up most of the convoy. As time passed the pranks became more and more comical and bizarre. In Wyoming the two staged an elaborate hoax that the convoy was about to be attacked by rampaging Indians. The official expedition scribe was so taken in by this ruse that he would have reported the matter to the War Department had not Eisenhower and Brett intercepted his telegram at the last moment. Yet another prank took place one night when Brett climbed a bluff behind the bivouac area and howled like a coyote. Scarcely a night went by without one or the other devising some devious scheme to bedevil the city slickers. Eisenhower thought their escapades were "part of an audience for a troupe of traveling clowns."[12]

In North Platte, Nebraska, Eisenhower was reunited with Mamie, Ikky, Pupah, and Nana, who had driven from Denver to meet the convoy. From Nebraska to Laramie, Wyoming, the Eisenhowers spent their first time together in nearly nine months. By the time it ended in San Francisco on Labor Day, 1919, the expedition had been seen firsthand by an estimated 3.25 million people. After gala festivities in Oakland, the participants paraded through the streets of San Francisco to the accompaniment of cheers and whistles blowing from ships in the bay. The mayor presented the keys to the city. "They had a big dance and a show at the St. Francis Hotel. Girls put on burlesque dances which caused the mothers to take their daughters home. The mothers then came back to see the show and dance with the soldiers."[13]

The expedition was officially disbanded in San Francisco, and each participant returned to his own home station. The journey had taken sixty-two days, a mere five days behind the original timetable, a remarkable feat in early-twentieth-century American history. The official report noted that the expedition had suffered 230 road accidents, including breakdowns, delays, mud, and quicksand, most of them minor. The army's image was enhanced, and many valuable lessons were learned that were incorporated into the future design of military vehicles. Awareness of the expedition reached an estimated 33 million Americans and helped to spur several state legislatures to begin enacting bills to build new roads.[14] Thirty-seven years later President Dwight Eisenhower would sign into law one of his highest priorities, the Interstate Highway Act of 1956, which created the Eisenhower Interstate Highway System.

. . .

Eisenhower was granted a month's leave and accompanied Mamie and Ikky from Denver to San Antonio, where they would remain for several months before moving to Maryland. For a brief time during the summer of 1919 it had been a time of adventure that Eisenhower termed "a journey through darkest America."[15] There would be precious few such free-spirited occasions during his military career.

13.

A Friendship Forged

From the beginning he and I got along famously.

When he returned to Camp Meade in the summer of 1919, Eisenhower finally met Colonel Patton, the officer who was to have such a profound effect on his military career for the next twenty-five years, and who would both "delight and dismay him for the rest of his life."[1] Patton commanded the light tanks of the 304th Brigade, while Eisenhower was second in command of the 305th Brigade, composed of newly manufactured Mark VIII Liberty tanks, which had come off the assembly line too late to be used in France.

There was an instant affinity between the two men, who were nonetheless as different as night and day. Patton was a decorated combat veteran with a Distinguished Service Cross who had single-handedly organized the AEF Tank Corps and been gravely wounded on the first day of the Meuse-Argonne offensive the previous year. Five years older than Eisenhower, he had graduated from West Point in 1909. Patton seemed monumentally egotistical next to the more self-effacing Eisenhower, who was nevertheless particularly impressed by the incongruity of this impatient, self-confident, elegant soldier with his high, squeaky voice. Patton loved horses, riding, and polo, and both men were avid riders, hunters, and pistol shooters, although Eisenhower had no interest in polo. One was wealthy and could afford an extravagant lifestyle; the other was dirt poor and had difficulty making ends meet. For a time the two played poker together twice a week. One could afford to lose; the other continued to supplement his meager pay by his shrewdness at the table. One of Eisenhower's biographers has noted another significant difference: "Everybody thought from the beginning of Georgie's career that there were no limits to the heights he might achieve. For most of his life very few people thought that Eisenhower would achieve anything much."[2] Another has observed, "Tact became a way of life to Ike, whereas Patton (to paraphrase Winston Churchill on John Foster Dulles) was a bull who always carried his own china shop around."[3]

On balance they seemed a genuinely mismatched pair: the brash, outspoken cavalryman and pioneer tank officer, and the fun-loving midwesterner whose roots were in the infantry. Yet the two soon forged an enduring friendship that lasted until shortly before Patton's death in December 1945. As Eisenhower would later write, "From the beginning he and I got along famously. Both of us were students of current military doctrine. Part of our passion was our belief in tanks—a belief derided at the time by others."[4] Their strong conviction that the tank had a greater role in the army of the future than merely as a subordinate arm of the infantry, as it had been during World War I, would eventually land Eisenhower in career-threatening trouble.

Both thirsted for something more exciting than the bland peacetime existence of Camp Meade, where Eisenhower spent his leisure time gardening and perusing a Burpee seed catalog for entertainment. The highway to the main encampment had been plagued by a number of holdups, and their boredom led Eisenhower and Patton to undertake their own version of cops and robbers by bringing the bandits to heel. Armed with half a dozen pistols, they drove very slowly down the road in the hope that they would be attacked. According to John Eisenhower, "Dad always said, 'We wanted to see what a fellow's face looked like when he's looking into the other end of a gun.' They were both going to pull guns in different directions and fix this guy. They thought they were going to be a two-man posse on the blacktop road there, but nobody stopped them. They were both disappointed."[5]

At first there were no married quarters for Tank Corps personnel at Camp Meade, and Eisenhower lived in bachelor quarters until the autumn of 1919 when he was reunited with Mamie. He rented a wretched single room in a Laurel, Maryland, boardinghouse that was too tiny to include Ikky, who was left in Denver in his grandparents' care.

Eisenhower's home life at Camp Meade was a mirror image of his Abilene upbringing, where make-do and secondhand were bywords. The experience was taxing, and Mamie never forgot how "they would turn off the electric lights at 6:00 o'clock in the morning and not turn them on again until 6:00 o'clock at night." With no place to cook, the Eisenhowers ate their meals in a nearby boardinghouse. Ike was often on duty until late at night, while Mamie was left alone in a depressing, often dark room to cope as best she could. "That was a horrible time," she recalled. After several weeks her life had become so intolerable that she returned to Denver and the comfort of her family. "Ike begged me to stay," but Mamie told him, "Ike, I just can't take this any longer."[6]

The hardships of army life had clearly stretched the bonds of their marriage. Still smarting over his inability to serve in the AEF, and deeply hurt by his disastrous reunion and unhappy parting from Mamie, Eisenhower was disconsolate. Even more dismaying, Mamie wrote only infrequently and then rarely mentioned their son or her family. Desperate for information, Eisenhower wrote instead to Nana.

> Dearest Mother:
>
> I hear from Mamie so infrequently that I have no idea how you all are getting along . . . we are very busy, [but with so many tank corps slots left unfilled], we seem to be chasing ourselves in a circle. . . . Would you mind, when you have time, writing me about Ikky & daddy & yourself. . . . I try to be patient & cheerful—but I do like to be with people I love. . . .
>
> Devotedly, your Son.[7]

Mamie did not return to Maryland until May 1920, after the authorities magnanimously permitted some rundown barracks in a sandy corner of Camp Meade to be converted into family living quarters. However, the army declined to assist in any way and left the expense of remodeling and furnishings to be paid for by each occupant. Thus it was that Eisenhower and Patton—now neighbors—added the title of "handyman" to their résumés.

Despite Beatrice Ayer Patton's wealth, a bevy of servants, and an automobile, at times the Pattons too had to make do with whatever was available. George Patton scrounged the only paint available from the quartermaster, blue and yellow—which became the primary motif throughout. Bea Patton solved the problem of what to do with the latrine by "planting wandering jew and trailing ivy in the urinals."[8]

Eisenhower likewise put considerable effort into remodeling the barracks into a suitable home, which included a lawn and a white picket fence. He hired off-duty soldiers, and a great deal of hard labor went into turning their quarters into a reasonable semblance of a home, though he could barely afford the expense, nearly eight hundred dollars, a hefty sum in 1919.[9] His love of gardening and tilling the soil was manifested at Camp Meade, even though the place was mostly sand. The pleasing results were proof positive of Eisenhower's green thumb.

"We didn't have a stick of furniture," remembered Mamie, to whom the task of furnishing the place fell. "I took orange crates and made a dressing table. . . . I got some cretonne and little thumb tacks and covered up the orange crates." In a former Red Cross building classified as a "dump pile," Mamie located a beat-up chaise and a table for the living room. Ike said, "My God, Mamie, you're not going to keep that?" Mamie replied, "Yes, I like it—I got it off the dump heap." Their beds were two army cots covered in cretonne adorned with Japanese prints, which she had purchased by the yard to make drapes. Impoverished as they were, Mamie Eisenhower managed to make a home for her family in what were scarcely better than broken-down old wooden buildings covered with tarpaper, where "you could see the cracks and they were built right, square, bang on the ground."[10]

In 1919 the temperance movement brought about the Eighteenth Amendment and Prohibition. Eisenhower and Patton both avidly joined in the all-American pastime of distilling their own bootleg alcohol. Eisenhower concocted his own gin in an unused bathtub, while Patton brewed beer in a woodshed and stored the bottles in the covered walkway between his quarters and the kitchen shack. One evening there was a sudden noise that sounded like a machine gun. Patton instantly dived to the floor, and the cook began screaming in the kitchen. The beer had exploded. "Georgie got up, rather shamefacedly, and explained that it had sounded so much like hostile fire that he instinctively had taken cover." Bea Patton "laughed and laughed and called him 'her hero,' and he got very red."[11]

Patton's two daughters, Beatrice and Ruth Ellen, were enchanted by Mamie Eisenhower, whom they found "the most glamorous creature that ever appeared in our lives. She insisted, very daringly we thought, that we call her Mamie and not Mrs. Eisenhower, as she said she wasn't that old yet." Although Beatrice Patton disapproved of her children calling any adult by her first name, she could do little when Mamie insisted. "She drank a lot of iced tea, which she stirred by swirling it around in her glass. We thought this the ultimate in sophistication, and tried to do the same with our milk, with bad results."[12] Despite the budding friendship between their husbands, however, Beatrice Patton and Mamie Eisenhower were never close, and seemed to have in common only the trait of frailty.

Mamie and Ike entertained frequently both for visiting dignitaries and in conformance with army custom that decreed the social responsibilities of a senior officer. For a brief period in 1920, their painful separations behind them, the Eisenhowers spent perhaps the most contented months of their married life. Although Eisenhower's competitive fires had been dampened by the end of the war, now that he and Mamie had been reunited, he enjoyed the slower pace of peacetime life at Camp Meade. Both cherished a beautiful, delightful son who enriched their lives.

Whereas the urbane Beatrice Patton was an avid participant in life and a major influence in promoting her husband's career, she and other casual acquaintances never saw the tougher side of Mamie: a woman of wit and charm who, although mostly a quiet spectator, nevertheless believed a military wife played an important role in her husband's career. There were even rare occasions when she would speak out forcefully when someone she thought unworthy was unduly rewarded, once complaining that the wife of a newly promoted brigadier general was "simply awful." Yet despite her growing confidence and maturity, Mamie was nonetheless guilty of the occasional gaffe, such as the time, when asked by Secretary of War Baker what Eisenhower was good at, she replied that he was an excellent poker player. A livid Ike berated Mamie for not telling Baker that he was a fine soldier. Mamie had merely assumed everyone already knew that.[13]

Baby Ikky spent a good deal of his time in the Patton household. The children of Camp Meade loved to fish in a nearby ditch, using bent-pin hooks and grasshoppers for bait. One day Ikky returned to the Patton quarters with a fish he had just caught and asked Beatrice to cook it for him. By then the fish "was pretty run down," recalled Ruth Ellen. "Ma told us to go and play. Pretty soon she came out with Icky's fish on a dish; a piece of buttered toast under it; garnished with a sprig of parsley and a lemon wedge. Icky ate it in ecstasy. Ma told us later that she had opened a can of sardines and dressed one up for the occasion."[14]

When the National Defense Act became law in June 1920, the Regular Army was authorized 300,000 men, but only 200,000 were left from what had once been a gigantic force of 3.7 million. By January 1921 Congress mandated another reduction in enlisted strength to 175,000, and in June a further cutback to 150,000 men. The ax fell again the following year, when Congress decreed that the active army consist of no more than 12,000 commissioned officers and 125,000 enlisted men, a strength it remained at until 1936.[15] The army's principal mission was relegated to that of training national guard and army reserves. Eisenhower and Patton were among those who disagreed but were too junior for their opinions to matter. The entire War Department appropriation was established at about $300 million annually, and with the navy considered the first line of defense, the army's share was woefully inadequate to meet its needs. In 1922 the U.S. Army ranked seventeenth among nations with standing armies, and in 1933, the chief of staff, Gen. Douglas MacArthur, noted that what few tanks the army possessed (except for a dozen or so experimental models) were "completely useless for employment against any modern unit on the battlefield."[16]

Although Woodrow Wilson's personal utopian vision of peace was a fantasy, it was his vision of a postwar world in which peace reigned supreme that gripped the United States in the aftermath of the armistice. Wilson had taken Europe by storm as the living embodiment of a golden age in which war would be relegated to the history books. The creation of the League of Nations was to be Wilson's eternal contribution to the world. However noble its intentions and potential role as the world's peacekeeper, the League instead was relegated to the role of an inconsequential body of diplomats and politicians whose power was limited to the use of persuasion without force. As historian Robert Leckie observes, "Not even Woodrow Wilson could have envisioned . . . the death of the dynasties and the end of empires was to be so quickly succeeded by the day of the dictator."[17] The surviving veterans of the German army were bitter at what they believed was the perfidy of the Jews and the politicians. Many, including a former corporal named Adolf Hitler, vowed one day to avenge their betrayal at Versailles by the Weimar regime.

In the United States the terrible bloodshed in Europe had bred disinterest in future war. The great patriotism of World War I had, by the early 1920s, turned into a national mania of aversion to all things military, and to the symbol of war, the military establishment. A militant pacifism took seriously the notion that America had indeed fought "the war to end all wars." Veterans, who months earlier had been wined and dined as national heroes, suddenly found themselves shunned. As MacArthur's biographer D. Clayton James has written, "Wrenched by fears of radicalism, economic depression, and renewed entanglement in Europe's distresses, the American people yearned for conditions of tranquillity, innocence, and isolation."[18]

Demobilization occurred on such a massive scale that it managed to overshadow the purge of the Union Army after the Civil War. By the end of June 1919, the Regular Army had been reduced to a mere 130,000, including the troops still on occupation duty in Germany.[19] Woodrow Wilson's illusory belief that future wars could be prevented by the new League of Nations left the military little more than an afterthought in the Roaring Twenties. The peacetime army of the interwar years has been aptly described as "an island surrounded by a sea of uncaring, more often contemptuous civilians," who had little regard for men with nothing better to do with their lives than soldier.[20] To all but a handful of officers, their government seemed to care only about reverting the armed forces to their prewar size. The last thing anyone wanted to hear was talk of another war from professional soldiers. Men like Eisenhower and Patton thus became anachronisms, even within their own army.[21]

During congressional hearings in 1919 on a bill to reorganize the army both Secretary of War Baker and the chief of staff, Gen. Peyton C. March, argued for retaining the independence of the Tank Corps.[22] Just when there seemed to be hope, it was dashed a week later when Pershing testified that the Tank Corps "ought to be placed under the Chief of Infantry as an adjunct of that arm."[23] Rockenbach's lame arguments for an independent corps were too conservative and neither passionate nor persuasive at the most critical moment in the history of the tank service. In the end it hardly mattered. Pershing's towering reputation and his opposition sounded the death knell of the Tank Corps. A War Department mandate ensured that the corps would now lose its identity and with it, its raison d'être. For Eisenhower, Patton, Brett, and the other intrepid pioneers of the Tank Corps who comprised the "Treat 'Em Rough" Boys, it was a bitter pill.

The total authorization of the Tank Corps was established in 1919 at 154 officers and 2,508 enlisted men, and the dreaded (but expected) postwar demotions finally caught up with both Patton and Eisenhower in the summer of 1920. Eisenhower was demoted to captain but a month later was promoted to major. Patton too reverted to his permanent Regular Army grade of captain but was likewise fortunate enough to be promoted to major. Both officers were among only a handful to be so propitiously promoted. The army had indeed fallen on hard times.[24]

Just as the army was sliding to its nadir, their brief time at Camp Meade brought together two of the pivotal U.S. leaders of World War II. Both might justifiably have walked away from any responsibility for the future of a spiritless army. Fortunately its soul was held together by the dedication of these men and others like them, who argued that the tank ought to be more than merely an auxiliary arm of the infantry. As Eisenhower has explained, "George and I and a group of young officers thought this was wrong. Tanks could have a more valuable and more spectacular role. We believed . . . that they should attack by surprise and mass. . . . We wanted speed, reliability and firepower."[25]

By themselves they stripped a tank down to its last nut and bolt and managed to put it back together—and make it run. They tinkered with supporting weapons and endlessly debated tank employment and the tactics of surprise. One day they narrowly escaped death when a cable stretched taut between two tanks suddenly snapped and barely missed their heads as, at lightning speed, it cut a lethal path through the nearby brush and saplings, in what both acknowledged was one of the most frightening moments of either man's life. Patton likened it to his near-death wounding in the Meuse-Argonne, while Eisenhower later wrote, "We were too startled at the moment to realize what had happened but then we looked at each other. I'm sure I was just as pale as George. That evening after dinner, he said, 'Ike, were you as scared as I was?' 'I was afraid to bring the subject up,' I said. We were certainly not more than five or six inches from sudden death."[26]

Another time Patton was test firing a .30-caliber machine gun while Eisenhower observed the trajectory of the bullets through field glasses. Without warning the weapon "cooked" and began spewing bullets everywhere. The two future generals raced off in panic but returned to disable the gun with sheepish expressions on their faces. After this second near-disaster both decided they had about exhausted their luck. Nevertheless they kept at it within a small circle of converts, among them Serano Brett, learning lessons, analyzing tactics, and creating scenarios in which tanks were employed under a variety of situations and conditions. As Eisenhower later said of this period in their careers, "These were the beginnings of a comprehensive tank doctrine that in George Patton's case would make him a legend. Naturally, as enthusiasts, we tried to win converts. This wasn't easy but George and I had the enthusiasm of zealots."[27]

In 1920, Eisenhower and Patton each published provocative articles about tanks in the prestigious *Infantry Journal*.[28] Their articles were nothing less than a proposed tank doctrine for the next war. Eisenhower's article was titled "A Tank Discussion," and it stressed the need for a newly designed tank of the future, armed with two machine guns and a six-pounder main gun, able to cross nine-foot trenches and speed cross-country at twelve miles per hour. The clumsy, inefficient machines of Saint-Mihiel and the Meuse-Argonne were now relics of the past, and "in their place we must picture this speedy, reliable and efficient engine of destruction . . . in the future tanks will be called upon to use their ability of swift movement and great fire power . . . against the flanks of attacking forces."[29]

By combining maneuver with the traditional supporting artillery fire, Eisenhower and Patton began to make the case that well-designed tanks could maneuver en masse and either outflank an enemy position or, as Fuller suggested, tear gaping holes in an enemy line and precipitate the collapse of an entire front. The possibilities of such tactics were nothing less than breathtaking. In future wars the infantry would close on the enemy and hold them in place, while tanks enveloped and either destroyed them or set the stage for the infantry to win a decisive victory at a fraction of the cost in blood of the linear battles of the past.

For many years branch chiefs in the War Department administered the engineer, ordnance, medical, and quartermaster functions, but for the first time since the Civil War the National Defense Act reestablished these offices for the combat arms: the infantry, artillery, and cavalry. Each chief was a major general, and collectively the branch chiefs constituted what was known as the special staff of the War Department. These powerful men spoke for their particular service and were a virtual law unto themselves when it came to branch doctrine, research and development, and the control of personnel assignments. The Tank Corps had no independence, few friends in court, and was now at the mercy of the chief of infantry, Maj. Gen. Charles S. Farnsworth, who had no fondness for either tanks or the officers who commanded them.

What each had concluded was heresy to the leaders of the infantry, with its long tradition (and privilege) of being the decisive arm of war and the "Queen of Battle." What these two upstart tank officers were suggesting would alter the whole doctrine of land warfare. Some infantrymen regarded Eisenhower's article as blasphemy, and in the autumn of 1920 he was summoned to Washington for an unpleasant audience with Farnsworth, during which he was warned that his ideas "were not only wrong but dangerous and that henceforth I would keep them to myself. Particularly I was not to publish anything incompatible with solid infantry doctrine. If I did, I would be hauled before a court-martial. . . . George, I think, was given the same message. This was a blow. One effect was to bring George and me even closer."[30]

Eisenhower's verbal censure in 1920 for daring to advocate the study of tanks and the need to enlarge their role was a message that even the dimmest